CHRISTOPHER
SCOATES,
CURATOR

UNIVERSITY
ART MUSEUM,
UNIVERSITY
OF
CALIFORNIA,
SANTA
BARBARA

D.A.P. /
DISTRIBUTED
ART
PUBLISHERS,
NEW YORK

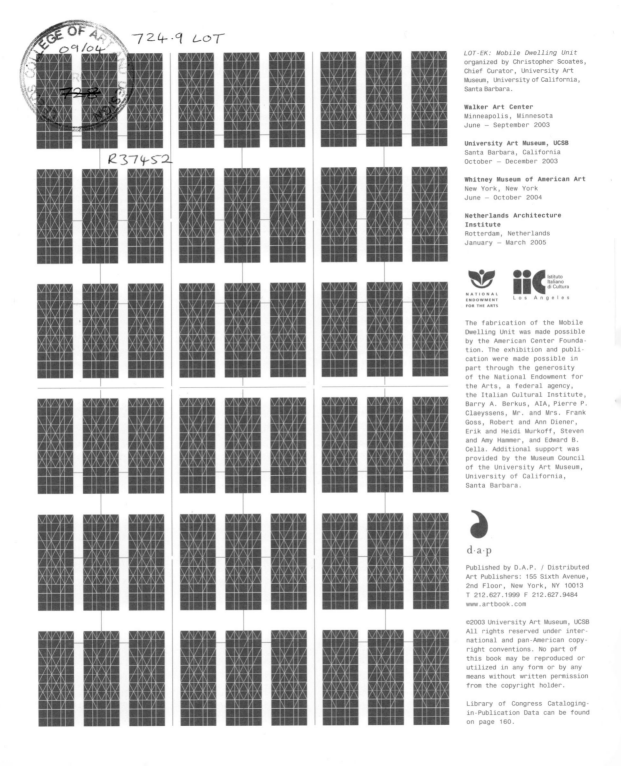

LOT-EK: *Mobile Dwelling Unit*
organized by Christopher Scoates,
Chief Curator, University Art
Museum, University of California,
Santa Barbara.

Walker Art Center
Minneapolis, Minnesota
June — September 2003

University Art Museum, UCSB
Santa Barbara, California
October — December 2003

Whitney Museum of American Art
New York, New York
June — October 2004

**Netherlands Architecture
Institute**
Rotterdam, Netherlands
January — March 2005

NATIONAL
ENDOWMENT
FOR THE ARTS

iiC Istituto
Italiano
di Cultura
Los Angeles

The fabrication of the Mobile
Dwelling Unit was made possible
by the American Center Foundation. The exhibition and publication were made possible in
part through the generosity
of the National Endowment for
the Arts, a federal agency,
the Italian Cultural Institute,
Barry A. Berkus, AIA, Pierre P.
Claeyssens, Mr. and Mrs. Frank
Goss, Robert and Ann Diener,
Erik and Heidi Murkoff, Steven
and Amy Hammer, and Edward B.
Cella. Additional support was
provided by the Museum Council
of the University Art Museum,
University of California,
Santa Barbara.

d·a·p

Published by D.A.P. / Distributed
Art Publishers: 155 Sixth Avenue,
2nd Floor, New York, NY 10013
T 212.627.1999 F 212.627.9484
www.artbook.com

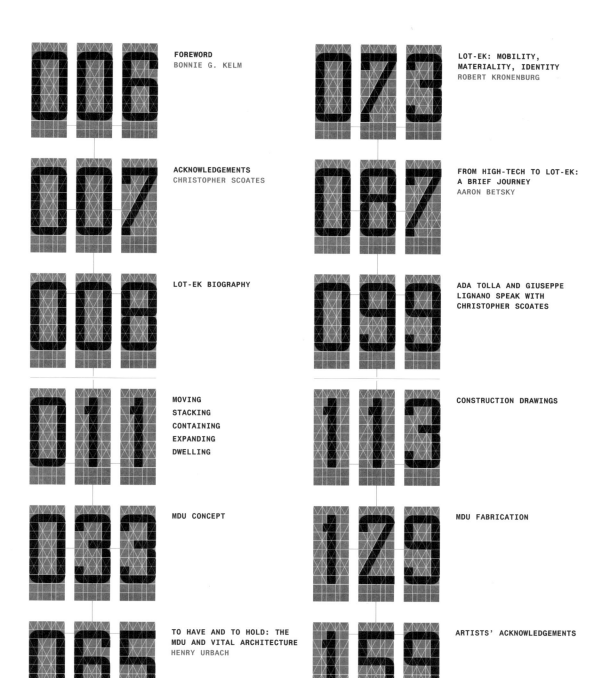

A prelude to becoming the new director of the University Art Museum at the University of California, Santa Barbara was my calamitous trip across country in a so-called "motor home." The discomfort of this experience prompted me to think about how wonderful a portable "home away from home" would be. It seemed prophetic to find, on beginning my tenure here, the LOT-EK MDU (mobile dwelling unit) had been commissioned by the University Art Museum in collaboration with the Walker Art Center.

Collaboration and promise are not only themes of this project; they also mark the alliances and processes that brought it to fruition. One of the hallmarks of the University Art Museum has been the integral relationship between the Museum's Fine Arts Collection and its nationally recognized Architecture and Design Collection. These two forces have shaped the collaborative and interdisciplinary focus of the Museum's exhibition programming, which often seeks to blur boundaries and transform expectations. We are always grateful for the creative synergy of the partnerships that are forged as we explore new exhibition possibilities. The University Art Museum is proud to have organized *LOT-EK: Mobile Dwelling Unit* and to have the exhibition open at the Walker Art Center, our generous partners in the project. We are also pleased to circulate the exhibition to the Whitney Museum of American Art and internationally to the Netherlands Architecture Institute, Rotterdam.

From the beginning, LOT-EK's MDU was a project passionately carried forward by the dedicated work of the Museum's Chief Curator, Chris Scoates. I am grateful to him for taking a leap of faith with this major work in progress. The vision and expertise of Andrew Blauvelt, Design Director at the Walker Art Center, was also essential to the realization of the project. We are indebted both to him and Alex DeArmond for the resonant design of this publication. Our appreciation is also expressed to Kathy Halbreich, Director of the Walker Art Center, for allowing us to share the Center's considerable resources. As with every major project of this complexity, there is always a vital supporting cast of people who make sure every aspect of the job is completed. I am thankful for the diligence of the University Art Museum staff in undertaking this important role.

The fabrication of the MDU would not have been possible without the support of the American Center Foundation. All those involved in the project are grateful for the Foundation's interest and major contribution. Significant support for the exhibition and publication was also provided by the National Endowment for the Arts. The Italian Cultural Institute and individual donations, as well as funds from the Museum Council of the University Art Museum, further enabled the realization of this exceptional project.

Most of all, we are tremendously grateful for the inspiration and creative brilliance of Ada Tolla and Giuseppe Lignano. At a time when it appears that industrial blight and material refuse have the capacity to overwhelm the human environment, the MDU prototype seeks to transcend conventional observations. LOT-EK projects do far more than propose solutions; they infuse our time with a spirit of optimism and sense of whimsical discovery. LOT-EK's unique approach to design serves to insistently remind us that endless possibilities are ever present.

Bonnie G. Kelm
Director
University Art Museum, UCSB

ACKNOWLEDGEMENTS

We at the University Art Museum, University of California, Santa Barbara (UCSB) take great pleasure in being able to host this exciting new project by LOT-EK, MDU (mobile dwelling unit). MDU is a provocative and experimental work that casts new light on the study and history of portable architecture. The rich history of experimentation and moveable architecture has been the focus of LOT-EK for the past decade. Using prefabricated and castoff industrial materials — petroleum trailer tanks, airplane fuselages, water tanks, and cement mixers — LOT-EK rethinks the ways in which people interact with the products and byproducts of our industrial and technology-driven culture.

It has been my pleasure to work closely with Ada Tolla and Giuseppe Lignano, the partners of LOT-EK, and Andrew Blauvelt, Design Director at the Walker Art Center, to develop the wide-ranging scope of the MDU project and catalogue. The Walker Art Center has a proven history of providing a platform for the most innovative artists working today. The University Art Museum, UCSB also has a history of presenting challenging contemporary art by emerging and established artists from around the country, albeit on a slightly smaller scale. In the best tradition of museum and artist collaborations, the University Art Museum, the Walker Art Center, and the principals of LOT-EK have combined talents and resources to make possible this distinct exhibition.

The organization of this project would not have been possible without the dedication of the University Art Museum staff. Chief among them is Director Bonnie Kelm, whose enthusiasm and dedication to the project was fundamental. Special thanks also to Kurt Helfrich, Curator of the Architecture and Design Collection. Susan Lucke, Registrar, was responsible for the smooth coordination of shipping. Exhibition Designer Paul Prince and Assistant Designer Rollin Fortier drew upon their years of experience to create the successful installation of the MDU project. Curator of Education Nicole Dewart's insightful programming in conjunction with the exhibition contributed to the interpretation of the project. Susan Jordan, Publicity and Marketing Coordinator, worked hard to "get the word out"; her efforts have paid dividends. Assistant to the Director Marie Vierra handled myriad tasks associated with the successful realization of this exhibition, as did Business Officer Victoria Stuber, who coordinated the funding and budgeting of this complex project. And Chief Museum Guard Reid Cederlof also deserves recognition for his assistance and good will. Last but far from least is Kathy Halbreich, Director of the Walker Art Center, who has been completely supportive of this project from the start.

As an academic institution the University Art Museum, UCSB stresses not only the educational function of its exhibitions, but also the professional training of students. During the several years required to prepare this project a number of student interns worked closely on the project, including curatorial assistants Shi Pu Wang and Kelly Turner. Both performed valuable research, executed correspondence, and assisted in numerous other valuable ways.

I extend particular gratitude and respect to catalogue essayists Aaron Betsky, Robert Kronenburg, and Henry Urbach, each of whose contributions here enliven the practice, discussion, and understanding of LOT-EK's work. Special thanks to Jane Neidhardt, with whom I've worked for years, and her long-time friend and collaborator Lee Sandweiss, who applied their exceptional editorial knowledge and expertise to mold four distinctive essays into a unified publication. And to Andrew Blauvelt, who not only helped shape the project but also designed with Alex DeArmond the catalogue, I express my continued appreciation for the style, grace, and exquisite sensibility that mark his work.

Finally, my deepest thanks go to Ada Tolla and Giuseppe Lignano, whose challenging and generous work inspired this collaboration. The same intelligence, attention to detail, sense of humor, and prescient critical observations that inform the work of LOT-EK have made working with them a truly pleasurable as well as rewarding experience.

Christopher Scoates
Chief Curator
University Art Museum, UCSB

LOT-EK BIOGRAPHY

LOT-EK is a New York-based architecture studio founded by Ada Tolla and Giuseppe Lignano in 1993. Born and raised in Naples, Italy, both Tolla and Lignano hold a master's degree in Architecture from the University of Naples, Italy (1989) and completed post-graduate studies at Columbia University, New York (1991). LOT-EK has achieved high visibility in the world of architecture, design, and art for its innovative approach to construction, materials, and space, and for its use of existing objects and technology as integral parts of architecture. Articles and reviews of their work have appeared in such publications as the *New York Times* Magazine, *Wallpaper**, *Domus*, *A+U*, *Wired*, *Surface*, *Metropolis*, *Vogue*, and *Harper's Bazaar*. Tolla and Lignano teach at the Parsons School of Design and have lectured widely across the United States and in England, Germany, Italy, Japan, Spain, and Switzerland. Their work has been exhibited and reviewed internationally.

LOT-EK PERMANENT

BUILDINGS - CULTURAL

2001
- Kowloon Cultural Center, Hong Kong (competition entry)

2000
- Students' Pavilion, University of Washington, Seattle (not built)

1999
- Deitch Projects Gallery, Soho, New York (not built)

1997
- Goree Memorial and Museum, Dakar, Senegal (competition entry with Florian Oberhuber)

BUILDINGS - COMMERCIAL

2002
- New World Trade Center, Max Protetch Gallery and Venice Biennale (concept)

2001
- Porta Susa Station and Tower, Turin, Italy (competition entry)

2000
- Container Mall, New York (not built)

1999
- TKTS Booth, Times Square, New York (competition entry)

1998
- Indoor Skateboard Park, Chicago (not built)

BUILDINGS - RESIDENTIAL

2002
- Clinton Square, New York (response to RFP with Costas Kondylis)

1999
- MDU Harbor, mobile dwelling units colony (concept)

INTERIORS - CULTURAL

2001
- The Bohen Foundation, Meat Packing District, New York

2000
- New Media Gallery, New Museum of Contemporary Art, Soho, New York
- Henry Urbach Architecture Gallery, Chelsea, New York
- Sara Meltzer Gallery, Chelsea, New York

INTERIORS - COMMERCIAL

2002
- WDDG, multi-media design office, New York (in progress)

2000
- Boon, clothing store, Seoul, Korea

1999
- Interface Showroom, San Francisco (not built)
- Klein Photography Studio, Meat Packing District, New York (not built)
- Management Artists, photo agency, Garment District, New York

1996
- LOT-EK Studio 2, Meat Packing District, New York

1994
- Produx, clothing store, West Village, New York
- LOT-EK Studio 1, Meat Packing District, New York

INTERIORS - RESIDENTIAL

2000
- Morton loft, West Village, New York

1997
- Macmillan penthouse, Soho, New York (not built)

1996
- Miller-Jones studio/residence, Midtown, New York
- Guzman penthouse, Midtown, New York

1993
- Bernstein apartment, Upper West Side, New York
- Alecci apartment, Chelsea, New York

LANDSCAPES

2002
- New World Trade Center Plaza, Max Protetch Gallery/Venice Biennale (concept)
- Gateway Plaza, University of Illinois at Chicago (response to RFP)

2001
- Kowloon Cultural Center Park, Hong Kong (competition entry)

2000
- Klein roof garden, Meat Packing District, New York (not built)

LOT-EK TEMPORARY

EXHIBITION DESIGNS

2002
- *Art Basel-Miami Beach*, video lounge, Miami Beach
- *AIA convention*, disposable stand, Edizioni Press, Charlotte, NC

2001
- *Bitstreams*, Sound-Channel, sound exhibition, Whitney Museum of American Art, New York
- *Making Time*, video exhibition, UCLA Armand Hammer Museum and Palm Beach Institute of Contemporary Art, Lake Worth, FL

2000
- *Ret-Inevitable 2.0*, projection space, Brooklyn Bridge Anchorage (not built)

1999
- *Ret-Inevitable 1.5*, projection space, Art 1999 Chicago
- *American Century II*, Whitney Museum of American Art, New York (design proposal)

1995
- *Recycle for the New World*, video theater, Museum at F.I.T., New York

EVENTS
2001
- Tema Celeste-Gabrius, launch party (not built)
- Summer's Warm Up at PS1, summer leisure at PS1, Queens (competition entry)
- Fashionlab, fashion show, Chelsea, New York

1999
- Fashionlab, fashion show, Dumbo, New York

1998
- Brooklyn Academy of Music, gala dinner for the Next Wave Festival

1997
- Brooklyn Academy of Music, gala dinner for the Next Wave Festival

1996
- Brooklyn Academy of Music, gala dinner for the Next Wave Festival

1995
- Performance Pavilion, Lorraine Kessler Gallery, Poughkeepsie, NY

SETS
1998
- DJ Tower, set for music video for A Tribe Called Quest

1996
- CBS News, sets for "Stuff," children's news show, New York (not built)

LOT-EK PRODUCTS

ARCHITECTURE
2002
- MDU, mobile dwelling unit prototype (in progress)
- WELCOME-BOX, Liverpool Biennial
- ESPN BUS STOP, bus shelter prototype for ESPN (in progress)

2001
- CONTAINER-CAFÉ, Art Basel—Miami Beach (delayed)

1999
- VISION-TUBE, Whitney Biennial, commissioned for Rockefeller Center (not built)
- MDU, mobile dwelling unit (concept)

1996
- AMERICAN DINER #1, restaurant chain prototype, Tokyo, Japan (not built)

FURNITURE
2002
- TELEMATIC TABLE, Walker Art Center, Minneapolis (invited competition)

2001
- LITE-SCAPES, molded rubber lighting units
- INSPIRO-TAINER, work/relaxation module, MoMA commission for Worksphere
- TV-TILE, modular television floor/wall/ceiling/counter system (in progress)
- LITE-GATE, light/surveillance installation, Hochberg-Healy residence, New York

2000
- MIXER, media cocoon
- SINK-WALL, pivoting storage system, Edizioni Press, New York
- CORD-LITE, lighting, Bernstein Showroom, New York

1999
- WORK-STATION, modular desk system, Management Artists, New York

1998
- TV-TANK, television lounging tube
- WORK-WALL, home/office wall unit, Ross/Bernstein apartment (not built)
- WIRE-LITE, dining light, Leiber residence

1997
- TV-LITE, modular television lighting system
- SURF-A-BED, multi-channel television surfing system

1995
- VIEWING-ROOM, "Eye to Eye," CBS News, New York
- WALL-THRU, units for home technologies (not built)
- POINT & SHOOT CHAIR, Vitra Design Museum, Weil am Rhein, Germany

1994
- CHROMO-LAMPS, detergent bottle lamp collection

1993
- BED/ROOM, convertible bedroom/living room
- ELECTRIC CHAIRS, microchips of human/technological functions
- FURNITURE COLLECTION, includes workstation, stereo lounger, conversation double seater

EXHIBITIONS - SOLO
2001
- *Urbanscanner*, Parsons Architecture School, New York

2000
- *MIXER*, Henry Urbach Architecture Gallery, New York

1998
- *TV-TANK: Television Lounging Tube*, Deitch Projects Gallery and Henry Urbach Architecture Gallery, New York

1994
- *LOT-EK Furniture Collection*, Barneys New York, Madison Avenue, New York

EXHIBITIONS - GROUP

2002
- *New World Trade Center*, Biennale d'architettura di Venezia, Venice, Italy
- *Architecture in Motion*, Vitra Design Museum, Weil am Rhein and Berlin, Germany
- *Synthetic*, Galerie Zurcher, Paris, France
- *Re-imagining Ground Zero*, National Building Museum, Washington, DC
- *New World Trade Center*, Max Protetch Gallery, New York

2001
- *LITE-SCAPES*, Henry Urbach Architecture Gallery, New York
- *Limites Borrosos 1:1*, Ministerio de Fomento, Madrid, Spain
- *TeleVisions*, Kunsthalle Wien, Vienna, Austria
- *Bitstreams*, Whitney Museum of American Art, New York
- *Workspheres*, Museum of Modern Art, New York

2000
- *Experiments in Architecture*, San Francisco Museum of Modern Art, San Francisco
- *Design Triennial*, Cooper-Hewitt National Design Museum, New York
- *TKTS 2K Competition*, Van Alen Institute, New York
- *Two by Two: Architectural Collaborations*, Berkeley Art Center, Berkeley

1999
- *VISION-TUBE*, Whitney Biennial, New York
- *3000 Chairs*, World Studio Foundation, New York
- *I'm the Boss of Myself*, Sara Meltzer Gallery, New York
- *TV-TANK: Television Lounging Tube*, CCAC Institute, San Francisco

1998
- *TV-LITE: Modular Television Lighting System*, Henry Urbach Architecture Gallery, New York

1997
- *SURF-A-BED: Multi-screen Surfing System*, Henry Urbach Architecture Gallery, New York
- *New York, New York: Materials for '96 Projects*, Material Connection, New York
- *A New Wave of Art and Design*, Los Angeles Municipal Art Gallery, Los Angeles, and Oakland Museum, Oakland

1996
- *The Perfect Chair for Barbie in the '90s*, I.C.F.F., New York, and Vitra Design Museum, Weil am Rhein, Germany

1995
- *Home Show*, Kessler Gallery, Poughkeepsie, NY
- *Celebrity Furniture Collection*, D.I.F.F.A., New York
- *Video Installations*, Here Theater, New York

1994
- *Hello Again! Recycling for the Real World*, Museum at F.I.T., New York
- *Extending the Boundaries*, Kessler Gallery, Poughkeepsie, NY

1993
- *New Directions 1993*, Poughkeepsie, NY
- *Transient Décor*, Horodner-Romely Gallery, New York

COLLECTIONS
- Guggenheim Museum, New York
- San Francisco Museum of Modern Art, San Francisco
- Private collections

AWARDS

2001
- Cooper-Hewitt National Design Museum, Environment Design finalist, New York

1999
- Architectural League, Emerging Voices Award, New York
- Vitra Design Museum, The Perfect Chair for Barbie in the '90s, Second Place, Weil am Rhein, Germany

MAJOR PUBLICATIONS

2002
- *Xtreme Houses*, Courtenay Smith and Sean Topham. New York and Munich: Prestel Verlag.
- *A New World Trade Center*. New York: Max Protetch Gallery and HarperCollins Regan Books.
- *LOT-EK: Urban Scan*. New York: Princeton Architectural Press.

2000
- *MIXER by LOT-EK*. New York: Edizioni Press.

1998
- *Loft*, Mayer Rus. New York: Monacelli Press.

MOVING
STACKING
CONTAINING
EXPANDING
DWELLING

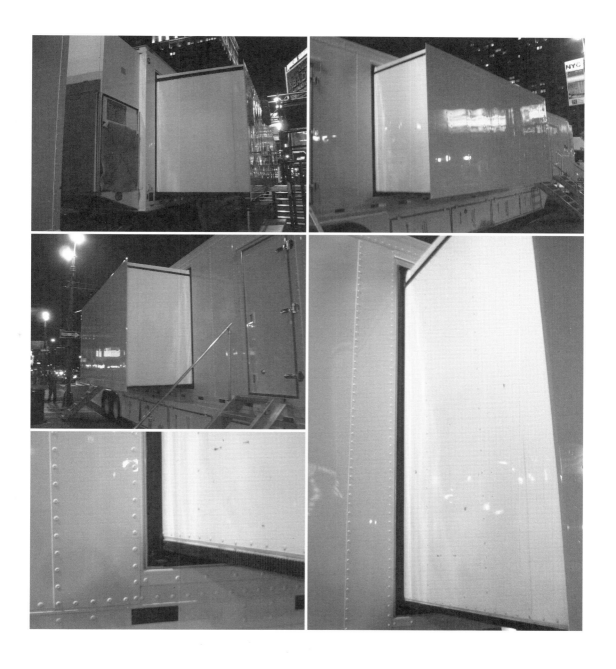

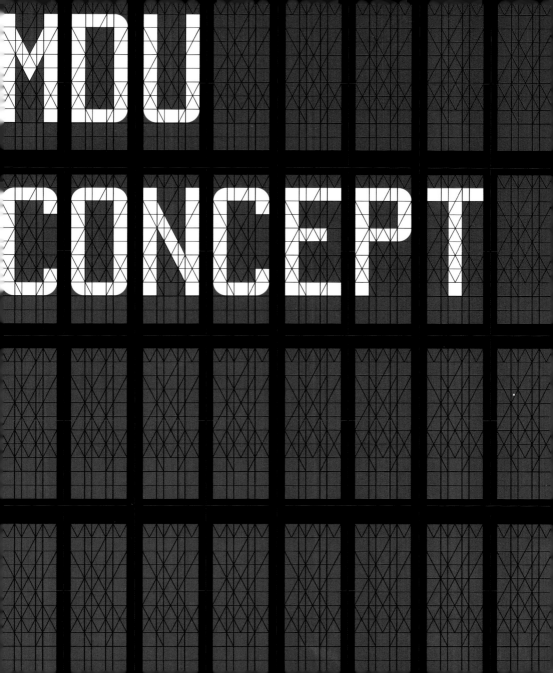

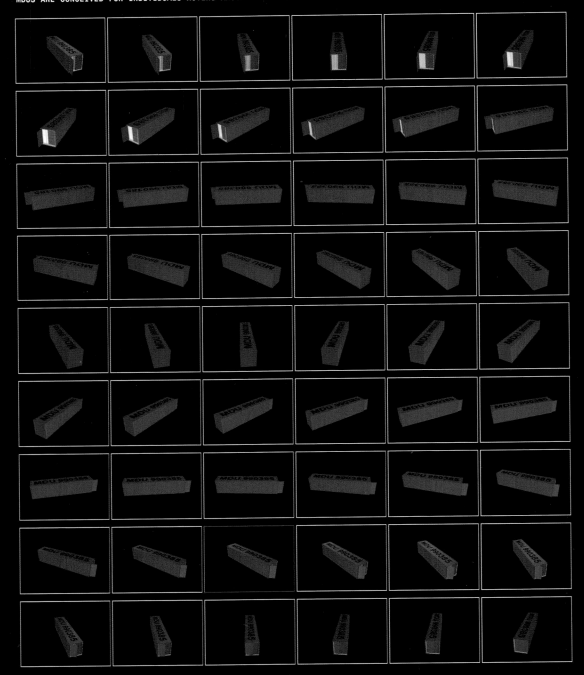

THE MDU TRAVELS TO MEET ITS DWELLER AT THE NEXT DESTINATION, FITTED WITH ALL
LIVE/WORK EQUIPMENT AND FILLED WITH THE DWELLER'S BELONGINGS.

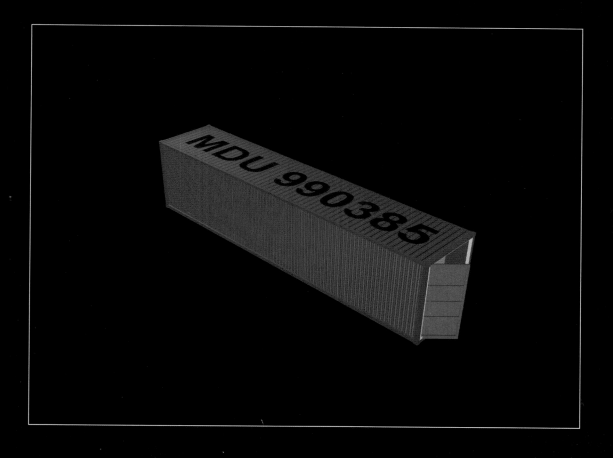

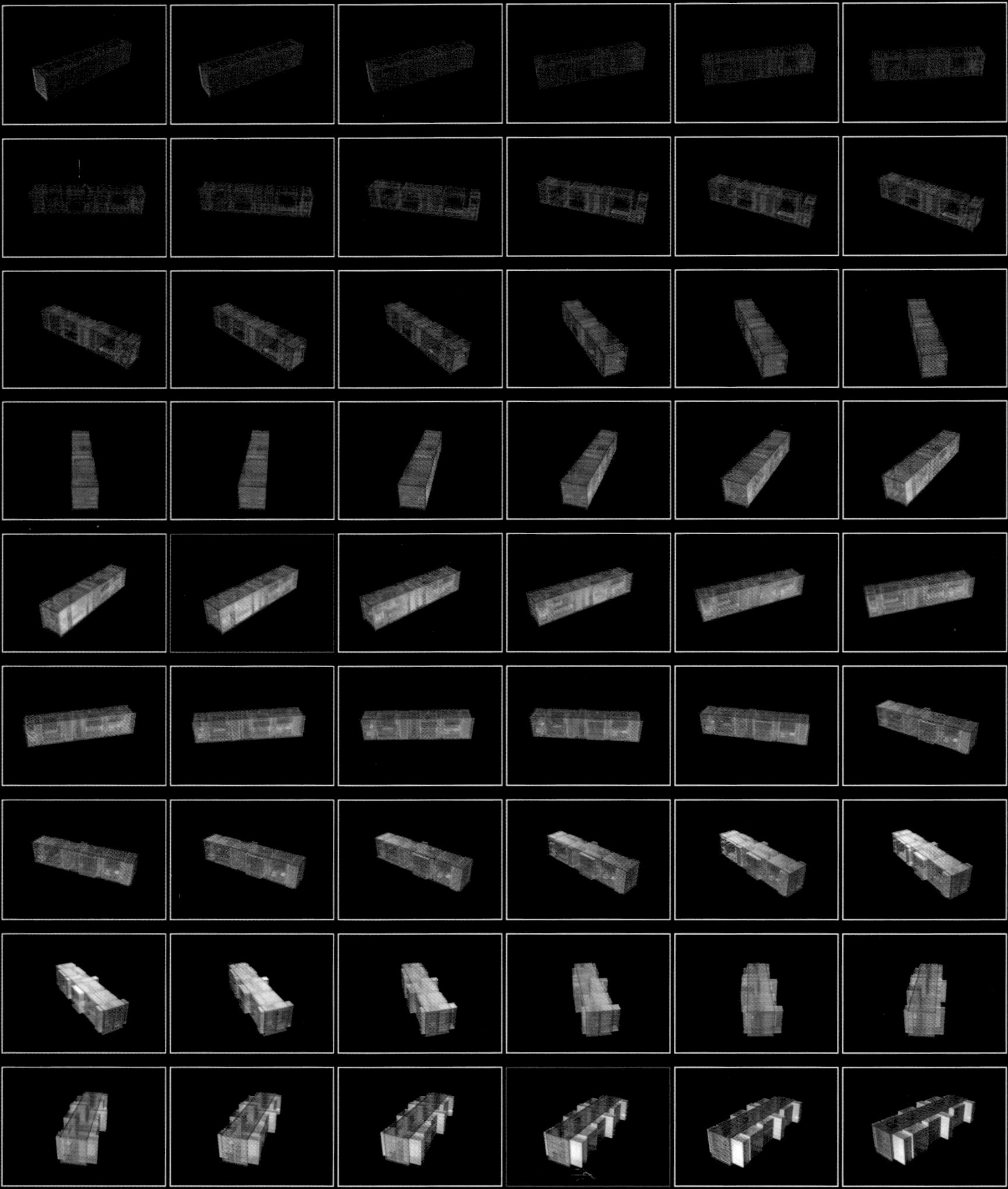

CUTS IN THE METAL WALLS OF THE CONTAINER GENERATE EXTRUDED SUBVOLUMES, EACH
ENCAPSULATING ONE LIVE, WORK, OR STORAGE FUNCTION.

WHEN TRAVELLING, THESE SUBVOLUMES ARE PUSHED IN, FILLING THE ENTIRE CONTAINER,
INTERLOCKING WITH EACH OTHER AND LEAVING THE OUTER SKIN OF THE CONTAINER FLUSH
TO ALLOW WORLDWIDE STANDARDIZED SHIPPING.

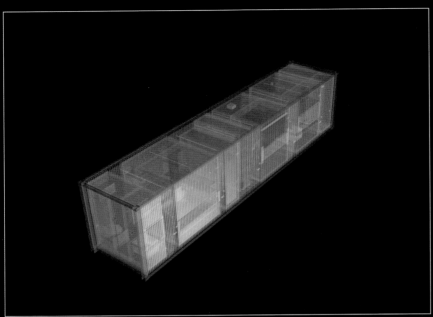

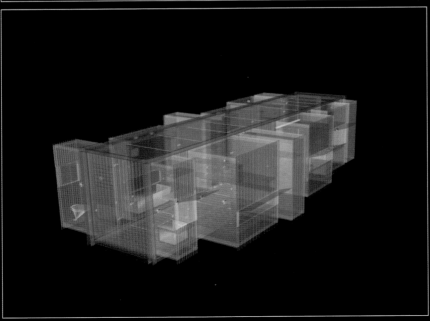

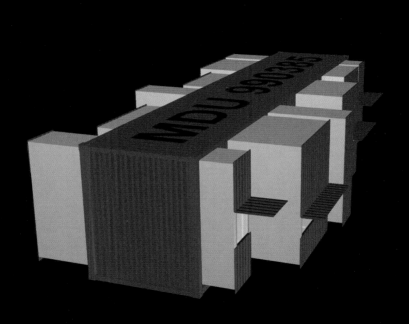

IN CONTRAST TO THE METALLIC EXTERIOR OF THE CONTAINER, THE INTERIOR SURFACES ARE FINISHED WITH NATURAL PLYWOOD. THE INTERIOR OF EACH EXTRUDED SUBVOLUME IS FABRICATED WITH BRIGHTLY COLORED PLASTIC-COATED PANELS. A FLUORESCENT LIGHTING SYSTEM RUNS ALONG THE LENGTH OF THE FLOOR AND CEILING. ROLLING BOOKCASES AND CLOSETS OPEN INTO THE CENTRAL VOLUME OF THE CONTAINER.

044

HE BUILT-IN FURNITURE OF EACH SUBVOLUME IS DESIGNED TO ADDRESS A SPECIFIC FUNCTION. THE SUBVOLUMES ARE POSITIONED WITHIN THE CONTAINER TO WORK TOGETHER IN PAIRS.

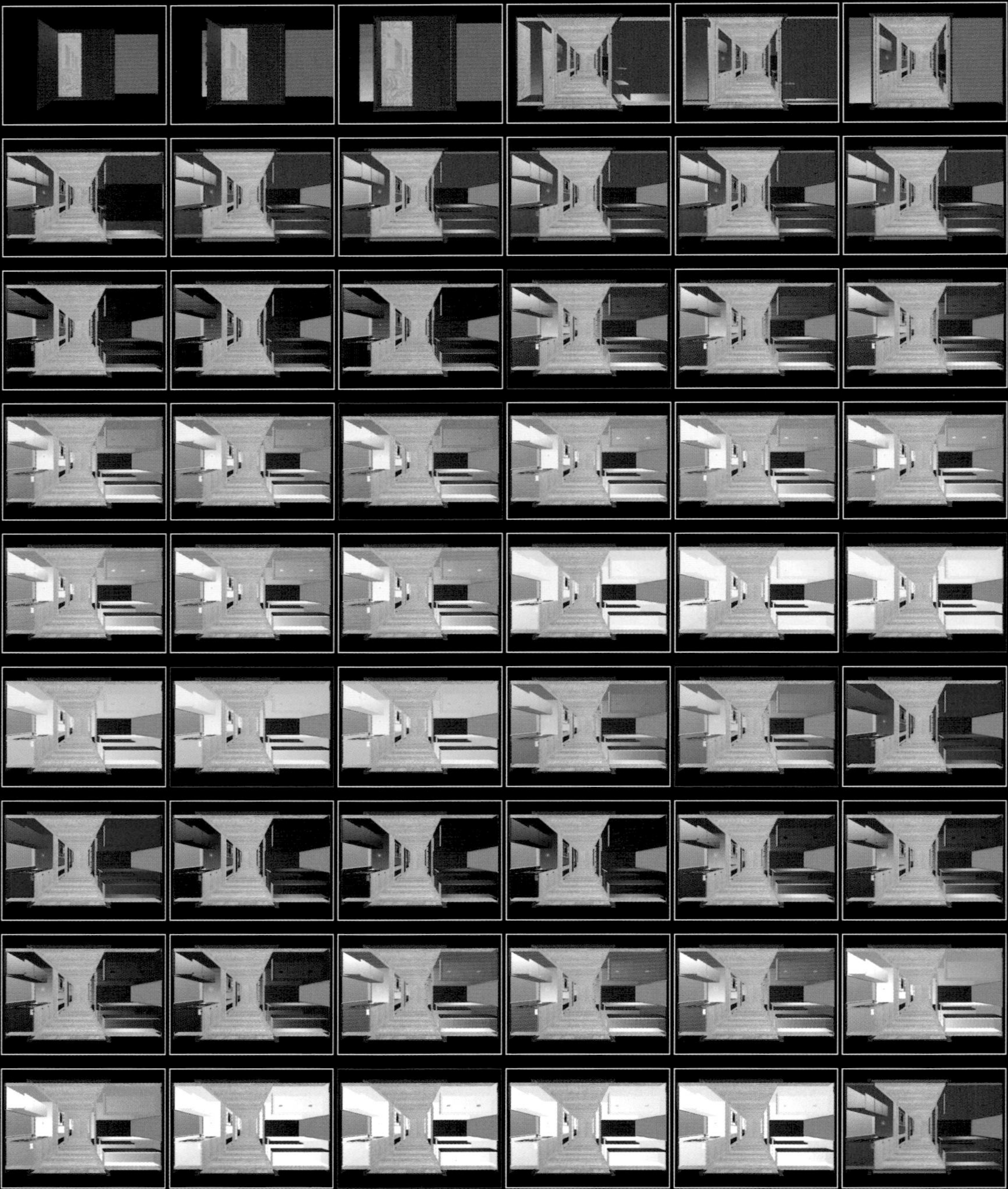

A SIMPLE METHOD OF CONSTRUCTION ALLOWS FOR A VARIETY OF CUSTOMIZATION OPTIONS. THE FINISH OF THE NATURAL PLYWOOD INSIDE THE CONTAINER AND THE COLOR OF THE PLASTIC-COATED PANELS LINING EACH SUBVOLUME CAN BE CHANGED TO SUIT THE TASTE OF THE MDU OCCUPANT. THE POSSIBILITIES ARE ENDLESS.

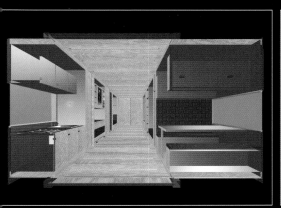

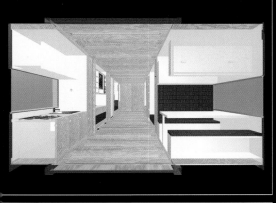

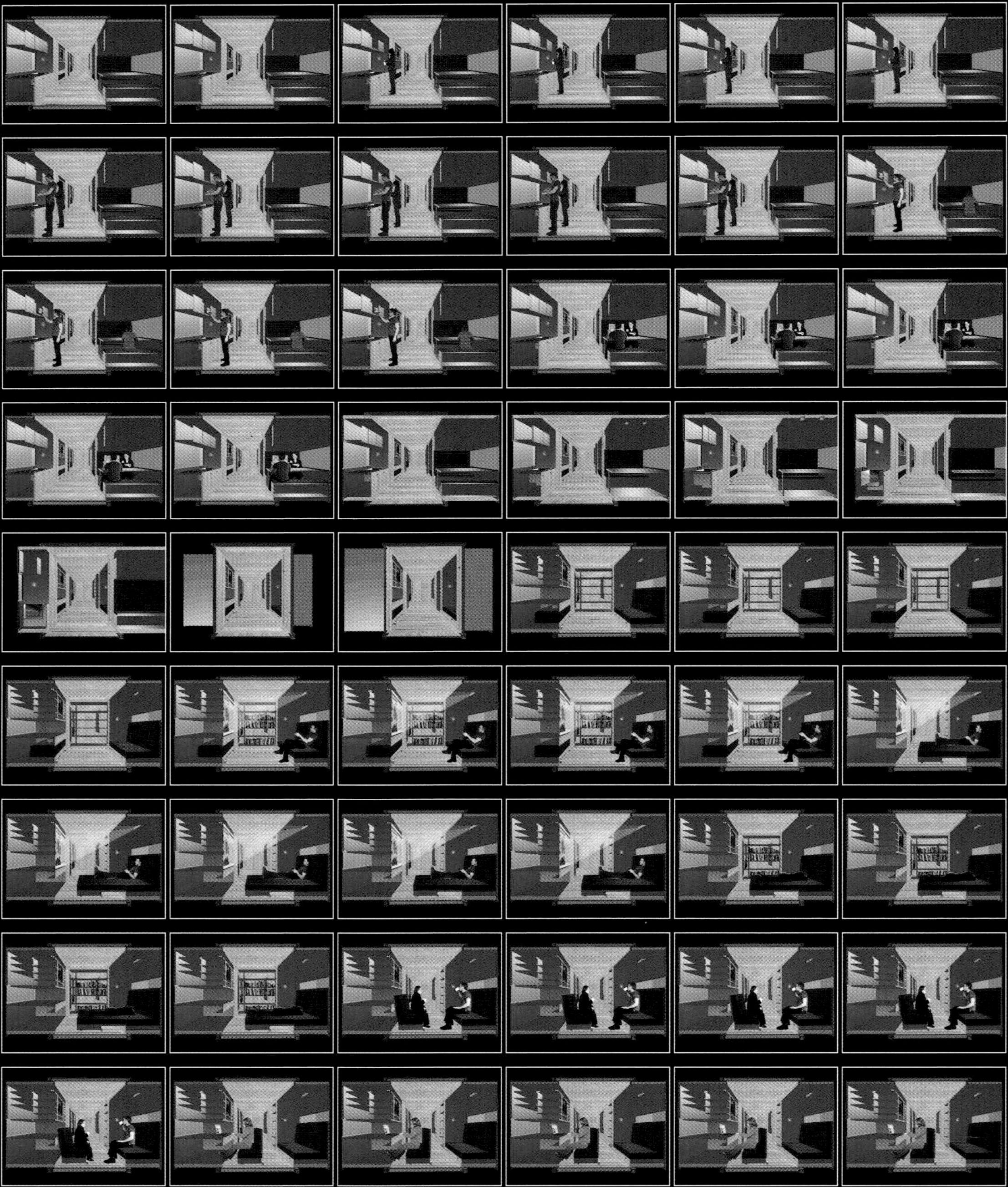

MORE SOCIAL ACTIVITIES, SUCH AS COOKING AND EATING, OCCUR IN THE FRONT OF THE CONTAINER
IN THE KITCHEN AND NOOK SUBVOLUMES. IN THE MIDDLE OF THE CONTAINER, THE SOFA AND
TV/DESK SUBVOLUMES FUNCTION AS A WORK AREA AND AN ENTERTAINMENT CENTER.

049

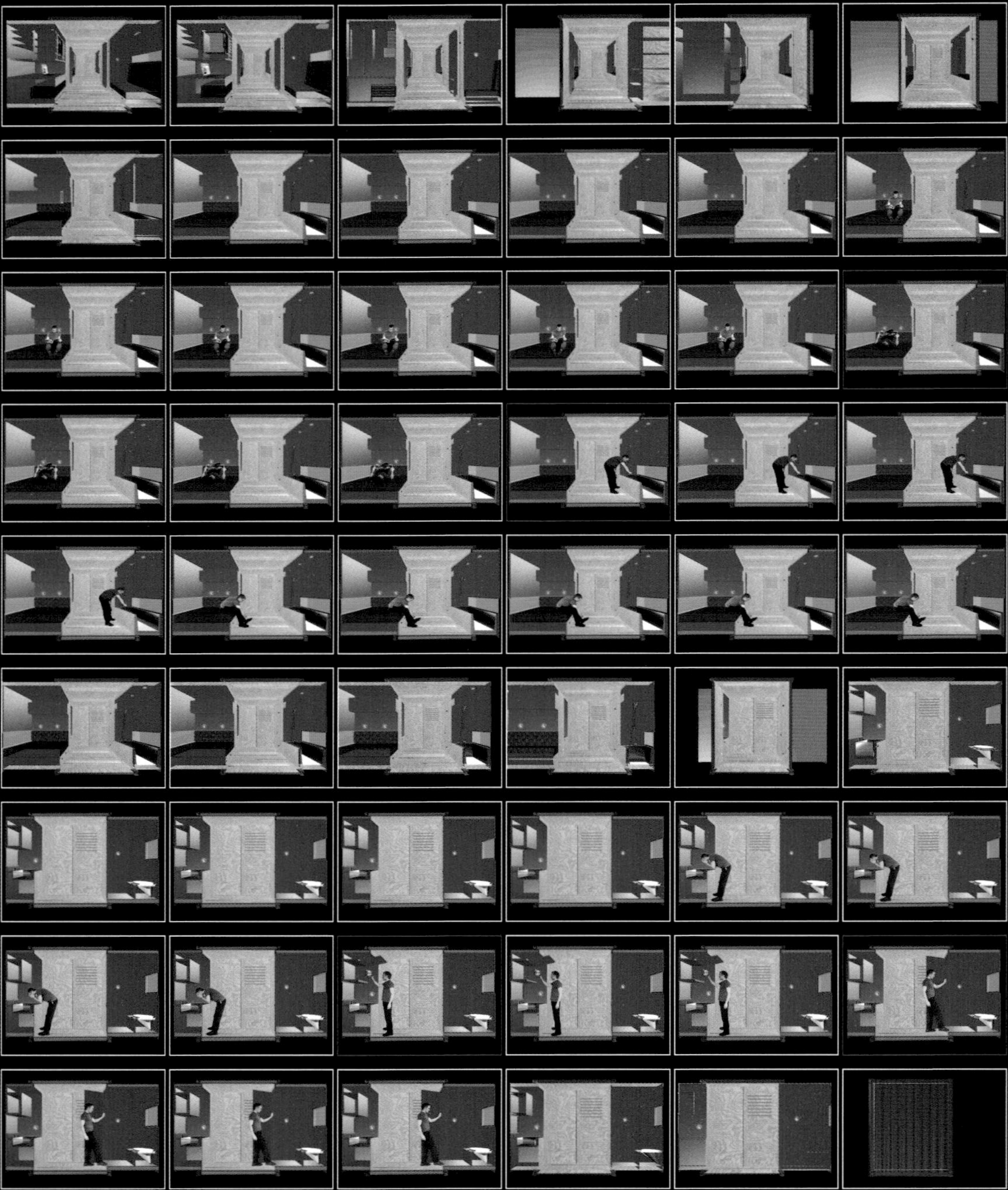

HE PRIVATE SPACES CONTAINING THE BEDROOM AND BATHROOM ARE LOCATED AT THE BACK OF
THE CONTAINER.

05

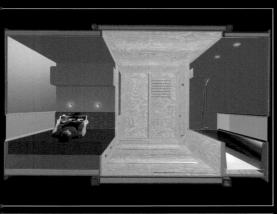

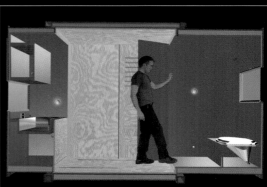

ONCE THE MDU REACHES ITS DESTINATION, IT IS LOADED INTO MDU VERTICAL HARBORS LOCATED IN ALL MAJOR METROPOLITAN AREAS. THE HARBOR IS A MULTIPLE LEVEL STEEL RACK MEASURING EIGHT FEET IN WIDTH (THE WIDTH OF ONE CONTAINER) AND VARYING IN LENGTH ACCORDING TO THE SITE. STEEL BRACKETS SUPPORT AND SECURE MDUS IN THEIR ASSIGNED POSITION, WHERE THEY ARE PLUGGED IN TO CONNECT TO ALL SYSTEMS. THE HARBOR'S STRETCHED LINEAR DEVELOPMENT IS GENERATED BY THE REPETITION OF MDUS AND VERTICAL DISTRIBUTION CORRIDORS. ELEVATORS, STAIRS, AND ALL SYSTEMS (POWER, DATA, WATER, SEWAGE) RUN VERTICALLY ALONG THESE CORRIDORS. TECHNOLOGY CONNECTS THE INTERIOR TO THE EXTERIOR WITH A SYSTEM OF REMOTE SURVEILLANCE CAMERAS AND MONITORS.

CRANE SLIDES PARALLEL TO THE BUILDING, ALONG THE ENTIRE LENGTH, ON ITS OWN TRACKS.
IT PICKS UP MDUS AS THEY ARE DRIVEN TO THE SITE AND LOADS THEM INTO SLOTS ALONG THE
RACK. THE VERTICAL HARBOR IS IN CONSTANT TRANSFORMATION AS MDUS ARE LOADED AND
UNLOADED FROM THE PERMANENT RACK.

LIKE PIXELS IN A DIGITAL IMAGE, TEMPORARY PATTERNS ARE GENERATED BY THE PRESENCE
OR ABSENCE OF MDUS IN DIFFERENT LOCATIONS ALONG THE RACK,

062

REFLECTING THE EVER-CHANGING COMPOSITION OF THESE COLONIES SCATTERED AROUND
THE GLOBE.

063

TO HAVE
AND TO HOLD:
THE YOU
AND VITAL
ARCHITECTURE

The studio of LOT-EK, situated at the western edge of lower Manhattan, holds a meeting area wrapped with artifacts that inspire the team's projects: containers of all kinds, maps, postcards, cell phone packages, bits of hardware and, near the windows overlooking the postindustrial riverscape, a sign advertising ice cream by the Italian company Algida. The poster depicts about a dozen different confections — vanilla cones dipped in chocolate and covered with nuts, disk-shaped ice cream sandwiches, popsicles on a stick — sweets of all kinds spinning around a longhaired nymph rising out of the blue sea.

In the course of many visits to LOT-EK's studio (we met in 1996, when I was asked to write about the Miller-Jones studio for a design magazine, and then became friends and collaborators), I have often wondered about this sign. Is it a way that Ada and Giuseppe maintain their link to childhood summers along the Bay of Naples? Is it a kind of color chart, filled with sunny hues one rarely sees so far from the Mediterranean? Or, as I have come to think more recently, is it a map, a way of thinking about architecture as a technology for producing pleasure? Might this sign function almost as a talisman, to inspire the firm's work, as well as to remind us how play and its rituals of spontaneity can be considered a guiding principle of design? The ice cream sign, I've come to believe, serves to stake a claim for joy in a vital contemporary architecture.

LOT-EK's MDU (mobile dwelling unit) emerged as an experimental design project, at once speculative and intended for realization, in late 1999. The basic proposition was to take a forty-foot container from a supply of already existing containers used in the shipping industry and transform it into an individual home that could be readily transported through existing transportation systems and set up in other locations. From the very first stages of the project, the MDU was also meant to join with other MDUs in quasi-urban conglomerations LOT-EK calls "MDU Harbors." A specific kind of living environment, reduced in area yet rich with spatial and technological possibilities, the MDU was designed to help individuals better integrate with the demands and opportunities of life in the early twenty-first century.

As with LOT-EK's earlier projects that use ready-made containers (including the AMERICAN DINER #1, TV-TANK, MIXER, and the Morton loft, all of which we'll visit shortly), it would be unwise to consider the MDU as an effort to recycle materials in a strictly ecological sense. LOT-EK is interested in what its founders have called "artificial nature" — the world as a conglomeration of natural and constructed phenomena — and their appropriation of ready-made objects derives from this premise. Shipping containers are contemporary analogues to stone or timber; they exist near at hand and ready for use. As LOT-EK takes castoff elements of industrial and electronic processes and restores them to the realm of the animate, it revitalizes these remnants, wresting from them a capacity to function as elements of architecture.

Consider one of LOT-EK's early projects, the AMERICAN DINER #1 (Figs. 1, 2), designed in 1996. Already with this unbuilt work, the studio articulated many of the ideas later elaborated in the MDU. Two shipping containers were transformed and coupled to form a habitable and programmatically specific architectural space. One container holds cooking facilities, the other a counter and dining area, with a long horizontal window formed by cutting the container and folding the excised band of metal. A supergraphic, AMERICAN DINER #1, wraps the entire exterior of the container, integrating the identification and promotion of the object with its architectural surface. The diner can be shipped and located anywhere, and its modularity allows for different configurations as local conditions vary. With the AMERICAN DINER #1, LOT-EK established a procedure for making a formal/programmatic hybrid, forcing castoff industrial forms to meet radically different programmatic demands, and allowing new life to spring from this collision. Moreover, with the AMERICAN DINER #1, as with the MDU, the building itself is treated as a kind of suitcase that can be tagged, transported, and set down again with contents intact.

With TV-TANK (Fig. 3), presented at Deitch Projects Gallery in 1998, LOT-EK took on the challenge of not only designing, but also building a work of revitalized architecture. Here LOT-EK cut, shaped, and retrofitted the interior of a thirty-five-foot-long aluminum petroleum trailer tank to create a television viewing lounge. The tank was cut into a set of thirty-inch and sixty-inch-wide rings, each lined with foam and rubber tubing and fitted with one or two televisions and remote controls. Inside the belly of the tank, viewers reclined in a kind of gravity-free suspension and enjoyed both the tubular perspective of

Figs. 1, 2: AMERICAN DINER #1
Tokyo, 1996

Fig. 3: TV-TANK
Deitch Projects Gallery/Henry Urbach Architecture Gallery
New York, 1998
photo: © Paul Warchol

interior space and the profusely animate flicker of hundreds of channels of satellite TV. With this project, LOT-EK met the hard and stubborn realities of working with the postindustrial container and began to develop a language for analyzing, cutting, and refitting it to make an environment suitable for habitation. Though it was developed at a very different scale, TV-TANK can also be seen to follow from the studio's early experiments with detergent bottles, which were cut open and filled with light bulbs and electrical wiring, then reassembled to create standing lamps that emit colored light.

If the program for TV-TANK was relatively reduced — a viewing environment suitable for lounging and watching television — programmatic challenge of the Morton loft (Fig. 4) was substantially greater and moves us closer to issues of domestic life at play in the MDU. Here, within a Manhattan loft they also renovated, LOT-EK again introduced a petroleum trailer tank into a space where it did not belong. The tank was sliced open to create twin sleeping pods that hover loft-like above a living space. The capsules, fitted with electronically operated hatches and night-time reading lamps, figure as womb-like spaces that nestle intimate activities within the overall space of the apartment. Traces of the tank's former life — adhesive marks from decals and stickers, pipe fittings, warning lights — remain on the exterior, to ensure that the appropriated artifact never entirely assimilates to its new context, but rather sustains a dialogue between what was and what is.

The MIXER project (Figs. 5, 6), presented at my gallery in 2000, likewise misappropriates a container (here a twelve-foot concrete mixer) and, through a set of subtractive and additive procedures, renders it a kind of multimedia cocoon. Viewers climb into the hollow interior and lounge on watery blue foam while selecting from dozens of entertainment options displayed on twelve monitors: interior and exterior surveillance cameras, satellite television, a Sony Playstation with computer games, video and music discs, etcetera. Here, again, LOT-EK undertook the task of transforming an object once inert, foreign, and hermetic into one that is, instead, close at hand, intimate, and ready for action. The tough and pragmatic exterior of the container was again maintained to intensify, by contrast, the enriched experience within.

Fig. 4: Morton Loft
New York, 2000
photo: © Paul Warchol

Figs. 5, 6: MIXER
Henry Urbach Architecture Gallery
New York, 2000
Guggenheim Museum Collection
photos: © Paul Warchol

The architectural object, as it anticipates future life, can be seen as a kind of incubator. Let's consider the MDU as a specific kind of "holding environment," with reference to the writings of the British psychoanalyst, D.W. Winnicott. As we consider the utility of this concept for an analysis of contemporary architecture, we need to attend to the possibility that the task of the built object is to give care and sustain life, much like the relationship, so well charted in Winnicott's work, between mother and child. The designer's task, in this regard, would be to ensure that the built object is organized to provide for the care of its inhabitant, and to maintain this care over an appropriate period of time until the individual is prepared to move on.

In *Playing and Reality*, as well as other volumes of essays written over the course of the 1950s and '60s, Winnicott considered how productive relationships serve to nurture play and provide for the mutual experience of pleasure. The holding or facilitating environment, as he sometimes called it, the space between the mother and child, was productive if it allowed for this kind of play and depleted if it did not. For Winnicott, concerned with establishing principles of contemporary psychoanalysis, the therapeutic relationship could provide a holding environment analogous to that of early life, and thereby permit the patient to discover or recapture earlier moments of play and discovery.

For Winnicott, mother and child are entangled in a process of mirroring one another to create a space that joins and separates them while structuring shared experience. How might we think about the relationship of bodies and buildings as a kind of mirroring, where the fitness, not only physical but also emotional and spiritual, of one body is received and reflected back by the other? Inextricably entangled, the couple of architecture and inhabitant would together mark out a terrain of possible experience, ranging from the depleted and dry to the lush and spontaneous.

Stubbornly, LOT-EK takes defunct artifacts of industry, containers for things, and invests them with the capacity to sustain life and activate experience. Tanks, mixers, shipping containers: it requires a tremendous commitment of resources to locate and find ways to use these bits of artificial nature. As they do so, LOT-EK establishes a scene analogous to that of psychoanalysis, taking the reduced and rigid and enlivening it with a new capacity to structure experience. Objects once castoff, literally piles of junk at the edges of cities, become newly familiar. Containers become incubators as they are selected, captured, and injected with new programs and spatial orders that sustain a productive and playful relationship with the human body.

Enter the MDU. A specific sequence is offered, a particular way of dwelling. The extruded volume, its proportions curiously between those of a conventional hallway and room, organizes a passage from most public to most intimate activities that marks out a diurnal cycle: arriving, cooking and eating, working and viewing, resting and bathing. The container divides along its length into two balanced halves, each holding moveable subvolumes that contain program and equipment in such a way that they can be collapsed for transport and opened outwards to ready the MDU for use. These smaller volumes are fully expressed along the MDU exterior when occupied and not, as they might easily have been, wrapped by an outer skin that would unify and conceal them.

Along one side are volumes that hold equipment. These are met, across the central passageway, by spaces to which they are programmatically and spatially linked: cooking-dining, media-sofa, bed-bath, sink-toilet. Each dyadic pair is articulated clearly in sections through the structure. A definite push-pull is established repeatedly along the length of the MDU, relationships of interdependence marked and held in a dynamic balance. These lateral connections are emphasized by two sets of hyphen-like lines, slots of recessed fluorescent lighting that cross the floor and ceiling, as well as grooves that guide the sliding subvolumes. A generous number of closets and cabinets line the edges of the container, including a deep closet that appears just beyond the entry door. These closets not only provide storage but also perform the symbolic function of reiterating, as boxes within a box, the logic of the holding environment.

In all of its container projects, LOT-EK has established a dialogic relation between the container surface and care of the inhabitant. This approach was first articulated in the Miller-Jones studio (Figs. 7, 8), where, to separate private and public program within a live-work loft, LOT-EK inserted a huge sheet metal wall, taken from the side of a truck; imbedded within this wall were all kitchen appliances, storage, and cable television. Consistently, the skin of the appropriated container is invested with what we might call life-support systems, elements that

Figs. 7, 8: Miller-Jones Studio New York, 1996
photos: © Paul Warchol

serve and support the inhabitant. In both TV-TANK and MIXER, the skin was thickened to hold cantilevered television sets; in the MDU, likewise, the skin opens and slides to contain all equipment and appliances. Through this newly equipped surface, human bodies pass and inhabit spaces once reserved for inanimate objects. In the MDU, this thick surface becomes a double skin, with refurbished steel on the exterior and plywood inside, which the individual can paint or otherwise modify as desired.

LOT-EK's commitment to enriching and sustaining the individual's relation to his or her living space can be understood by looking at two other projects, each for different reasons. The Goree Memorial and Museum proposed for Dakar, Senegal (see p. 95), uses shipping containers to create a museum of the African slave trade. To mark the extreme dehumanization of this historical period, LOT-EK treated the shipping containers as building blocks rather than incubators. Containers are joined in a monumental megastructure, then cut to create a range of spatial volumes that visitors move through. The primary relationship of individual to container is set aside here in favor of representing what happens when human beings are reduced to an abstract relation of property and exchange. Instead of directing us inward, LOT-EK moves us towards an experience akin to entering the hold of a ship, a "holding" environment that remains utterly depleted.

Compare this arrangement with LOT-EK's design for MDU Harbors, also megastructures made of shipping containers, intended for major metropolitan areas around the globe. A multilevel steel rack, adapted from the structures actually used to store shipping containers in port, the MDU Harbor allows for the semipermanent placement of individual units, while providing essential services such as electrical power and water. One container in width and as long as necessary, the Harbor does not encourage spatial interaction between horizontally and vertically adjacent MDUs; each individual unit tenaciously maintains its inward focus. More a dynamic and dense agglomeration of individuals than a community or collective, the MDU Harbor represents the self-determination of the twenty-first century global nomad and insists on his or her wish to dwell in a particular and private way.

A look at one final LOT-EK project, the Students' Pavilion (Figs. 9, 10) intended for the University of Washington in Seattle, reveals an effort to create a more collective holding

Figs. 9, 10: Students' Pavilion University of Washington Seattle, 2000

environment within another kind of container. Here, LOT-EK proposed to transform a sixty-foot-long section of a Boeing 747
fuselage into a student lounge. A clever, rotating floor/seating
system and a perimeter lined with projection surfaces would
fully animate the interior and make it suitable for many different kinds of events: lectures, screening, performances, parties,
and lounging. A tremendous range of spatial and programmatic
play is set in motion as students gain the means to figure and
reconfigure their own spatial and digital environments.

Sadly, this project was aborted after the events of September
11, 2001, when it no longer seemed appropriate to the university
to house its students in a slice of airplane. Whatever meanings
the airplane might have had before that day, and whatever meanings it might come to accrue, at a certain moment in time, it
could not shed its association with threat and danger. Winnicott
wrote about something like this when he discussed the child's
experience of abandon as a depressed mother turns away, the
experience of being dropped and let go. Stillborn by fear, anni-
hilated by worry, the Students' Pavilion can no longer serve to
incubate other activities, to anticipate and care for that which
is still to come.

A built work of experimental architecture, especially a work
pitched at the level of the MDU, is a kind of miracle. Against
all odds, against the deadening force of the normative and its
codification in design, legal, and construction practices,
experimental architecture stakes a claim to test the unknown.
Such work may succeed or fail, and will most likely do some of
both, but its ultimate significance resides elsewhere. A project such as LOT-EK's MDU stands for the possibility of human evo-
lution and claims that architecture can play a vital role in
structuring the spatial, social, and technical conditions of
this process. As it enters the world on its exhibition tour, and
possibly advances to become a new kind of home, the MDU opens
itself to interpretation, allowing us to test the claims of its
makers, and to imagine what might happen if.

LOT-EK:
MOBILITY.
MATERIALITY.
IDENTITY
ROBERT
KRONENBURG

July 2002 — LOT-EK's WELCOME-BOX (Figs. 1, 2) for the Liverpool Contemporary Art Biennial opens to the public. A standard shipping container, still showing the dents and scrapes on its tough steel shell, its original paintwork only partly masked with black and yellow hazard tape and Biennial lettering, sits besides the London platform at Liverpool's Lime Street railway station. It is a comparatively large and substantial object, but it is dwarfed, not only by the sleek intercity diesel that pulls in alongside it, but by the station itself, a massive nine-teenth-century engineering feat of iron and glass, built when Liverpool was second only to New York as the greatest port in the world. Now Liverpool's remaining port activities are based seven miles to the north, in a terminal where a handful of men operating machines manipulate containers such as this.

The shipping container is a familiar image in this industrial landscape, usually seen passing by on a low-loader, or stacked in rows at freight terminals and distribution warehouses. There is a workshop in the city where old shipping containers are converted to mobile site and storage huts; however, the inside of this one is very different from those — simultaneously dark, shiny, and vibrant, with the floors, walls, and ceiling either mirrored or covered with a black springy rubber surface. Strange sounds and images are pumped into the space isolating the occupant briefly from the noisy station outside. The special character of this internal environment cannot be imagined from outside, although there are hints: video monitors in individual steel boxes project from the side of the container and, at each end, there is a yellow ramp and handrail that invites entry. LOT-EK (which is architects and designers Ada Tolla and Giuseppe Lignano) has chosen the form and location of this, the first installation of many art-based projects that will be built in Liverpool before the end of the year. Intended as a gateway and a welcoming gesture to the city and its Biennial event, it is simultaneously both a familiar and a mysterious object. It is art, but it has function — perhaps, therefore, it is also architecture. Given that it arrived overnight and can be moved easily, it is also portable architecture. Portable architecture has a number of advantages in solving a task such as this: it can be placed on a site normally not available for building (because it is not permanent); there are no restrictions regarding its appearance (because it does not have to "fit in"); and its arrival is

Figs. 1, 2: WELCOME-BOX
Liverpool, 2002

both an event and a surprise (because it is prefabricated and its installation takes a short amount of time).

If the WELCOME-BOX is a surprise to the unsuspecting Liverpool-bound train travellers, it also has some surprises for those familiar with the history of its creators. For Tolla and Lignano, who trained in architecture at the University of Naples, this is their first built project in Europe. Another first for LOT-EK, which established its reputation by using industrial objects to create architecture and environments, is that this is the first installation to be realized using an intact shipping container, though the concept has figured in earlier projects.[1] AMERICAN DINER #1 (1996; see p. 67) was a design for a transportable theme restaurant to be installed initially in Tokyo. The Deitch Projects Gallery in New York used containers to define café and entrance spaces. Also in New York, the design for the Bohen Contemporary Art Foundation (2001; Fig. 3) features two containers that slide along tracks to create moveable and changeable exhibition spaces. LOT-EK's entry for the 1997 competition for a slave trade memorial and museum in Dakar, Senegal (see p. 95) is perhaps the firm's most ambitious project. Although essentially a static building, it consists of a megastructure, hundreds of meters long, constructed entirely from shipping containers — a linear, monolithic pier anchored in the city, but jutting out into the ocean, the containers enclosing exhibition and experiential spaces but also, in themselves, symbols of world trade. The megastructure LOT-EK has in mind now is one that moves.

Mobility

The MDU (mobile dwelling unit) is a shipping container transformed into a dwelling that nevertheless remains shippable. The MDU is a discrete mobile element that can be relocated into a new static infrastructure, the MDU Harbor, which is standardized around the globe. The MDU is a fully serviced interior environment with push-out elements for sleeping, storage, cooking, and bathing that are secured in the container when it is in transit. The dwelling is intended to follow its owner from place to place, carrying all their possessions, and is slotted into a transitory community for the duration of their residence in a given part of the globe. The MDU makes use of existing container manufacture,

1 The Miller-Jones studio (1996) used the side of a shipping container as a two-dimensional wall element (see p. 70).

Fig. 3: Fabrication of containers for Bohen Contemporary Art Foundation New York, 2002

handling, and transportation technology to make a (potentially) viable mobile dwelling that alters and extends the genre of the motor home, the caravan, and the trailer house.

LOT-EK's concept is to take an industrial object that already has global acceptance and find a new use for it. More than this, it has turned an industrial object — something that is appreciated for its usefulness and practicality — into a building that also has a range of other complex associations connected to human identity, meaning, and ambition. The container becomes a house, the base for our domestic life. The house is undeniably the most significant place in which we establish who and what we are. For most of us, it is the only building in which we have an individual right to be (as we select, rent, or own it ourselves) as opposed to using an office, shop, school, and so on. The house is the foundation of our existence, the place we have chosen to "be," and of course, human "being" is very important! The house is also the quintessential work of architecture — the source of all building design.[2] Building might be described as something made to simply fulfill a function, but architecture is more than this, and it cannot be denied that a dwelling, however humble, with all the emotional baggage it carries, must be identified as architecture. Besides, houses are so often the vehicle for architectural experimentation simply because they are homes: that form of building to which every human being can relate on a common level of understanding, need, and desire. The Villa Savoye, the Schröeder House, the Lovell House, the Eames House, Falling Water, the Farnsworth House, et al. were designed not only to house individuals but to make a statement about a way of living. The MDU is undoubtedly architecture; and, as it is designed to move from place to place, it is also portable architecture.

Surprisingly, portable architecture is not something new, but has been around since people started making buildings. Indeed, the first buildings were undoubtedly portable, because the first people were hunter-gatherers who needed to move year-round to ensure their continued supply of food. Contemporary portable architecture is in a transitional phase. As new materials and techniques become available, the option to build a portable rather than a static building is becoming more viable and more competitive. Even so, every type of building function has already been accommodated in portable form — education, medicine, commerce, industry, government, entertainment, housing —

2 Architect Wes Jones comments in his statement for the Archilab 2000 exhibition, Orléans, France, 2000: "The house is the architectural problem degree zero. All architectural programs are houses-for-something…." For further investigation of this topic see the author's essay "Modern Architecture and the Flexible Dwelling" in *Living in Motion, Design and Architecture for Flexible Living*, exhibition catalogue, Vitra Design Museum. Weil-am-Rhein, Germany: Vitra, 2002.

all have significant portable examples. In fact, we are so used to portable architecture being around that we generally don't see it unless it is pointed out to us and instead think of camping trailers and the Portakabin as the primary image of this building type.[3] However, ocean liners are vast floating mobile hotels with thousands of residents and workers. The circus (and rock concert, ice show, etcetera) is a mobile auditorium. There are mobile factories in the Antarctic, mobile offices at every expo and business convention, mobile hospitals and garages wherever there is a natural disaster. There is even a mobile laboratory in space.

Mobile housing is one of the most familiar forms of portable building. The caravan is a familiar icon of romantic dwelling, adopted as a realistic mode of life by some, but regarded by most as a peripheral design form. The North American mobile home, now relabelled "manufactured housing" to avoid connotations with the cheap, low-grade accommodation of the past, provides more than a quarter of all new homes in the US. However, this product is primarily about industrial prefabrication rather than mobility — once sited, mobile homes rarely move again. Nevertheless, there is a link here with LOT-EK's design, as prefabricated, moveable dwellings possess great economic advantages compared to conventional on-site construction, both in terms of cost and quality of build.

Other experimental designers have exploited both the advantages of prefabrication and mobility in housing. In the 1940s, Buckminster Fuller's impatience with a world that used its resources wastefully led him to adapt and reuse the Butler Bin, a grain storage silo, into the Dymaxion Deployment Unit, a simple but effective shelter. Though only two prototypes were ever built, his postwar Dymaxion House caught the imagination of the public: 37,000 orders were placed with the Beech Aircraft Company, which planned to convert their military plane factories to peace-time aluminum house manufacturing.[4] After the Second World War, 130,000 prefabricated, portable houses were built in the UK, and it was these, as well as Fuller's ideas, that were among the inspirations for the Archigram group to explore the issue of the mobile dwelling during the 1960s.[5] Archigram's intention was to reinterpret the concept of housing in a new way, drawing on innovative technologically-based ideas from engineering, the arts, and space exploration. Ron Herron's Walking City

3 Portakabin is the epitome of the familiar, lightweight, road-delivered office accommodation. It is interesting, however, that Portakabin subsidiary Yorkon has been working with the UK housing association, The Peabody Trust, and Cartwright Pickard Architects to develop high-quality, modular, prefabricated housing.

4 For a detailed examination of Fuller's work including the Dymaxion House and the reasons it failed to make it to the mass market see Joachim Krausse and Claude Lichtenstein, eds., *Your Private Sky: R. Buckminster Fuller, The Art of Design Science* and *Your Private Sky: Discourse*. Baden, Switzerland: Lars Müller, 1999.

5 The 1960s saw a wide range of experimental architecture groups emerge throughout Europe and North America, including Missing Link in Vienna and Ant Farm on the US West Coast, but Archigram, because of their potent imagery, communicated most effectively through the journal they produced, were the most influential.

(1964), a huge mobile urban center that moved from place to place, was inspired by the mobile platform that carried the giant Apollo space vehicles to the launch pad. Michael Webb's Cushicle (1966) and Suitaloon (1968) were personal dwellings inspired by the space suit, carried around by the wearer-inhabitant or a specialized small vehicle. However, it is Peter Cook's Plug-in City (1964) and Warren Chalk's Capsule Homes (1964) that are the most relevant precedents for LOT-EK's MDU.[6] These projects were part of a developing set of ideas that the whole Archigram group worked on between 1962 and 1966, exploring the notion of a motive urban environment where a flexible infrastructural framework would not only enable, but encourage, the development of an ever-changing city matrix. Pods containing houses or parts of houses could be moved at will within the infrastructure by cranes situated at the top of the grid. Movement demand was based on obsolescence of the pods (technology or fashion) and the desire for relocation. Plug-in City's energy was derived from the juxtaposition of all the varying mobile elements and the ad hoc way in which they would interact. Capsule Homes was an attempt to create a completely prefabricated dwelling that could be stacked into a tower. This project presented the idea that housing could be made from highly sophisticated components assembled into a single unit, which could then be interchangeable with others that are physically identical.

These and other Archigram projects were hugely influential on architects of subsequent generations, such as Richard Rogers and Renzo Piano in Europe and Kisho Kurokawa and the Metabolists in Japan.[7] However, built architecture that approaches the dynamic flexibility of Archigram's proposals simply has not happened. Rogers's and Piano's masterpiece, the Centre Pompidou in Paris (1971-77), is a homage to Plug-in City in appearance and intentions, but despite a recent refit, this multipurpose arts center has remained largely the same since it was built. The cranes on top of Rogers's Lloyds Building in London (1978-86) operate the cleaning system rather than load and off-load new building spaces. Besides, these buildings, though they contribute to a vibrant city environment, are not housing. The dwelling pods in Kurokawa's Nagakin Capsule Tower in Tokyo (1972), while undeniably in the spirit of Warren Chalk's sophisticated mass-produced predecessor, are stacked on top of each other and impossible to move.[8] Other capsule homes exist in some specialized situations. The Capsule Hotel is one of the cheapest forms of overnight urban

6 Others were Ron Herron's Gasket Homes (1965), David Greene's Living Pod (1965), David Greene and Warren Chalk's Drive-in Housing (1965). See *Archigram*. Basel, Switzerland: Birkhauser Verlag, 1991.

7 Another influence was London architect Cedric Price who, in 1961, designed the Fun Palace, an interactive, flexible building. Many ideas from the Fun Palace were incorporated into one of the first truly easily changeable, plug-in buildings, the Kentish Town Inter-Action Centre (1972) which utilized predominantly prefabricated components such as scaffolding, industrial site-huts, and a built-in travelling crane to make a local community center.

8 Kurokawa did do other nondwelling projects that adhered to the spirit and imagery of the plug-in concept, notably the Takara Pavilion at Expo '70 in Osaka, Japan.

accommodation in Japan: prefabricated plastic tubes just big enough to lie down in, complete with built-in TV and air-conditioning, are stacked in racks with adjacent lockers for clothes and communal washrooms. Usually located on several floors of a building that might also have other diverse uses, these accommodations are found primarily in the urban pleasure districts for hardworking office workers to sleep off their nighttime excesses. In London, escalating property costs have priced key service workers out of the housing market. The "micro-flat" has been proposed as a solution: a prefabricated, fully-serviced, studio/bed module placed into a specially designed permanent building, though the innovation here is more in the ownership strategy than construction or logistics.[9]

Californian architect Wes Jones's recent experiments with containers and other modular systems attempt to make a new form of housing that is derived from the technology used to make it, rather than applying technology as a symbolic imagemaker. In a range of individual house designs created since the late 1990s, Jones has examined the idea of the home as a mechanical container for the functions of living and working. Though the houses are static in terms of site, they do have mobile elements within them such as the sliding walls and moving bridge that accesses the storage areas of the Brill.1 residence (1999).[10] Jones also has no hesitation in utilizing the products of the commercial world as well as the industrial one. His PRO/con housing adopts the idea of consumer branding, such as is found with internationally known products like Nike, Porsche, and Calvin Klein, to the design and marketing of houses. This concept consists of an apartment infrastructure into which can be slotted standard size shipping containers outfitted by branded companies. The house buyer (who can perhaps more accurately be described as a dwelling consumer) buys into the brand in the same way that they buy their clothes, their car, and their jewelry — housing as accessorizing. Presumably changing logo, rather than location, would be the main reason for the units' mobility.

Despite all these interesting experiments, the really moveable, infrastructure-based, plug-in dwelling has yet to be built; but why not? And how might LOT-EK's project differ from previous projects in a way that makes it more likely to be realized? One reason is certainly that the necessary investment in a completely new housing system has been too much of a gamble. In this regard

9 The flat has restrictions on sale and resale that prevent wealthy purchasers from using them as a pied-à-terre or owners making a large profit when they move on.

10 Others are the High Sierras Cabins (1995), the Stieglitz residence (1998), and the Tsang residence (2000). The High Sierras Cabins project also uses modified standard shipping containers as a basic module in the construction.

LOT-EK's MDU proposal is based on tried and trusted technology that is already in place in every major port throughout the world, and people might more readily accept the idea that a container will stand up to the demands of transportation. Also, there is the problem of transporting large objects such as buildings. Weight is a universal issue in portable architecture, as transportation cost increases proportionally to dead load that must be moved. Surprisingly, however, there is no recognizable imagery for portable buildings; as with conventional architecture, they come in all shapes and sizes.[11] This is because of the issue of logistical practicality — extra weight is acceptable if there are other practical reasons that make transportation easy. If you only plan to transport on water, weight becomes less important. For example, sea forts built to protect the estuaries of English rivers during the Second World War were built from concrete and steel. Buildings built for road transportation are often constructed on a steel chassis stiff enough to take the rigors of the journey's bumps and jolts. The MDU is neither lightweight, nor inherently floatable, nor built with wheels. It is transportable because it takes advantage of a logistical system that is already in place in which relatively heavy loads have been accepted as a necessary part of the design criteria. The steel shipping container has been designed to provide its own structural integrity during handling and, in addition, protect its contents from damage. The industrial handling system has been designed to cope with this weight. The MDU takes advantage not only of the system that has already been developed for container relocation, but also the recognizable characteristic of the container as a moveable object.

Another reason for the curious lack of portable buildings is that it is uncertain whether people are able or willing to adopt a semi-transient lifestyle. Previously, they moved because it was necessary to move, because of changes in economies and industrial methods, population expansion, or in response to cataclysmic events such as war or natural disaster. Changes in work patterns brought on by information technology are leading to a global community that enables people to move between cities, countries, even continents and still find similar employment and recognizable cultural environments. It is now becoming more possible to work for an organization based remotely from where you live. People also relocate much more frequently for lifestyle or per-

11 Reduction of weight is a specialized area of design, utilizing new materials and new structural forms, and often resulting in remarkable imagery, for example, tension and pneumatic structures. However, these forms are just as likely to be found in innovative static building designs.

sonal reasons. Easy and instant communications and cheap global travel mean you can remain in contact with your friends and relatives. The concept of a moveable dwelling adds another facet to house-moving, as your friends and family can move too. For a time they might move to live by you, and then move on when the time is right.

The international hotel, delivering the same domestic image and standard of service that can be reserved on-line in any language, is currently providing a "home away from home" service to the traveller. Instead of providing an anonymous room in every port to the mobile worker, the MDU could provide a real home, their only home, in every port, with the added advantage of being based in a community of like-minded individuals. The MDU has two other architectural tricks up its sleeve. The first is its inherent anonymity on the outside, which, like a magician's trick, can be used to conceal a sumptuous, and highly personal, interior that has been customized to the owner's desire. Like a Swatch or an iMac, it is a mass-produced, yet simultaneously individual, expression of the owner's taste. Secondly, it presents the option of living in an apartment block in which one's neighbors are changing; for the longer term occupants, this amounts to a change of scene without going anywhere at all!

Materiality

It is not surprising that LOT-EK began developing its "reuse" approach to design after its partners' arrival in the US as visiting scholars at Columbia University. To a European, one of the first things noticeable about the American environment is how all-pervasive mechanical equipment is, and how it is so robust, substantial, and constantly in use. Machinery is on show: air conditioners poke out of windows; water towers sit on top of buildings; hydrants stand up out of the ground; and vehicles, especially trucks, are much bigger. These useful and sculptural objects help make up the pattern of urban America. LOT-EK talks of this urbanity as a new "natural" environment. So common and familiar, it is the contemporary version of the countryside — a street lamp as familiar as a tree, a traffic light as familiar as a bush, the pavement the grass, the road a stream. The objects found in this urban nature can be both inspirations and resources. If you are seeing an American garbage truck for the first time, believe me, it is impressive! Driving through the industrial zones of North American cities is like travelling through a vast candy store of objects, materials, and locations waiting to be found, recognized, and used.

LOT-EK design is architecture of the found object. It is the transformation of the industrially mundane into the uniquely beautiful. In using these objects, it is significant that LOT-EK does not generally attempt to tidy them up. Objects remain recognizable not only by their shape or materials but by the patina that remains from their previous life. The dents and scratches, faded paint, and signage are significant and important aspects of their beauty. LOT-EK reuses industry, but does not remake it. The fact that these objects have a recognizable history is important — it makes them specific, and releases them from their anonymity. When incorporated in a LOT-EK interior or installation the objects can be appreciated by people, who can get up close to them, in a new and intimate way. You get to know the tree in your own garden a lot better than the one in the forest; the container out of which your apartment is made is much more familiar than the one stacked in the shipping yard.

LOT-EK distances itself from the idea that reusing these objects is inspired by issues associated with recycling and sustainability. Rather than attempting to pursue design with a precisely calculated systematic agenda, LOT-EK simply makes use of what clearly already exists. Of course, this has economic and ecological benefits: previously used things are usually cheaper to buy than new ones, and using something without having to change it eliminates the whole energy burden of recycling. But these benefits would only be felt if large numbers of people start living in secondhand oil tankers and shipping containers. What these projects are really about is enabling us to recognize the beauty and value in everything we make, the old and the mass-produced as well as the new and bespoke. The idea is that by simply utilizing the benefits of portability and moving something to a new location, it can gain added value and usefulness. A shipping container, usually seen outside in a yard or on a truck, has a different and powerful presence when part of an art gallery interior.

There is also something a little disconcerting, out of context, and consequently stimulating about being in the presence of these relocated products. The use of found objects to make architecture provides an air of the reckless to LOT-EK's work, a sense of the happy accident, of the unforeseen juxtaposition. There is something surreal in relaxing inside the bowl of a cement mixer that appeals to the human desire for new experiences. It also reconnects with the concept of portability — an interior made from two-by-fours and plasterboard seems to be in its obvious, if mundane, place, but one made from used industrial components seems transient and temporary. The object's new function adds a sense of the temporal to its situation. If it is recognizable as an object that once served another role, who is to say it will not return to that in the future, or perhaps move on to something else? In designs such as the MIXER (2000; see p. 68) or the INSPIRO-TAINER (2001; Figs. 4, 5), this temporal quality is something to be valued rather than shunned, but it is also relevant in other fashion-conscious environments such as shop and restaurant design where it is imperative that the facility is current and "of-the-moment."

LOT-EK architecture is substantial. Perhaps this is a byproduct of the industrial objects it has chosen to reuse: steel containers, mixers, tanks. These objects are still around to be reused because they are tough, and that toughness is passed onto their reuse in a new situation. However, even when LOT-EK utilizes less powerful elements in a project, the end result still has a robust strength that suggests that this design can stand up not only to frequent use, but reuse, and ultimately relocation. The SINK-WALL (Figs. 6, 7) at Edizioni Press (2000) is shiny, lightweight, mobile, but still tough and industrial. LOT-EK's interiors reveal the texture of the existing structure as well as introducing new elements. The concrete, brick, or steel of the existing shell is often left in its found state — the patina, and therefore the history of the building, is at least partially revealed. A LOT-EK interior is an internalized version of the American external urban environment: no-nonsense, working, and workable. The designers' message is confident and, consequently, inspires confidence while it communicates stability and continuity. Surprisingly, this is synonymous with something uniquely American, the straightforward, "can-do" approach to life and work.

The honest, pragmatic, but surprising use of uncommon resources for building and object design also communicates ingenuity. It is not only stimulating to see things used for something they were not intended for, it is admirable — and it can also be amusing. It is admirable because it conveys a sense of efficiency

Figs. 4, 5: INSPIRO-TAINER
Commission for the exhibition
Workspheres
Museum of Modern Art
New York, 2001
photos: © Danny Bright

Figs. 6, 7: SINK-WALL
Edizioni Press
New York, 2000
photos: © Danny Bright

and economy. It is amusing because it is fun to see something done in a surprising manner: in recognizing the reused elements — fridges for desks, sinks for shelves — you enter into a collusion with the designers, recognizing and engaging with their agenda. Nevertheless, these simple recognizable objects, when converted, added to, and subtly (and not so subtly) changed, become something more than they were before. They can take on a new meaning. A single tessera may be an interesting object; however, it is only when it is united with many others to form a mosaic that its true identity is revealed. The individual MDU may be an example of the micro-scale of this project, but one has to imagine it as a part of a new flexible city environment to grasp the magnitude of the ambitions for the complete concept. LOT-EK's use of tough, often reused materials in an undecorated, unadulterated way connects with a whole range of aesthetic and cultural sensitivities — our yearning for history and stability; our desire to do more for less; and our need to understand and engage with the environment in which we live.

Identity

LOT-EK's partners trained as architects and perceive their work as architecture, though much of it transcends the boundaries of all areas of three-dimensional creativity. They craft furniture, light fittings, and domestic objects that are practical and meaningful. They create installations in art galleries that challenge artistic perceptions. They envisage ephemeral environments for special events. They build interior spaces in which people live and work. They design complex buildings that explore important issues about how we live in the world today. This multifaceted range of work is made possible by the path they have chosen to explore in their design work. It is a personal agenda and, despite the varied nature of the projects, is one that has a clear, continuing, developing basis. LOT-EK's ambition is the search for a new vernacular based on the products of industrial technology. These products are all around us, almost invisible, yet they form the interconnected machine that enables our urban society to operate. The idea that by making better use of the industrial infrastructure of the world we can change our lives for the better has been a recurring theme in design history. The designers, historians, and theorists who have explored this idea are legion — from William Morris to Wes Jones via Viollet-le-Duc,

Le Corbusier, Buckminster Fuller, Charles and Ray Eames, Archigram, Shigeru Ban, and others. LOT-EK's work consequently has resonance because it is part of an ongoing concern. It has further relevance because it consists of physical examples of how things with little or no value can be made into things of significant value. We might also then surmise that this work can be perceived as a comment on a consumer society, which almost universally aspires to the expensive and the new.

Architecture, like all arts, is referential. LOT-EK's reference, instead of the architecture of previous ages, is the industrial artifacts of today. The firm's architecture recognizes the precious nature of the mundane and how it fills the background of our environment but might, with a little effort, also be placed in the foreground. LOT-EK's work does not exhibit an excitement about the invisible, powerful technology (information technology and the science of new materials, methods, and systems) that is driving society and culture forward. It is about the physical, the visible, the tactile: the world with which we remain in contact — the new "natural" world. Although LOT-EK's work celebrates the physical world, it also incorporates the virtual world: video and audio systems are important parts of its installation work. However, by using powerful physical objects from which to view the media, LOT-EK's installations place the virtual world in perspective: when you step out of the MIXER, you are very conscious of regrounding yourself in the physical world. LOT-EK designs are clearly foils to high-tech, not examples of it.

These designs also can be perceived as a comment on society in another way. Their lack of conformity with the conventional image of architecture is a highly visible expression that they are made in a democratic society. Autocracies seek to control society and its creative acts, the form of architecture in particular being forced into patterns that express particular ideologies. Within a democracy it is possible to have a healthy disregard for what might be regarded as the "norm." A fundamental purpose of experimental architecture is to challenge conventional ways of doing things in order to explore alternatives, sometimes willful, sometimes wasteful, but usually vigorous and stimulating. Experimental architecture is an essential part of architectural development. Its effects usually take some time to filter through to the mainstream, but without them that mainstream would stagnate and become unresponsive to the changes in economics, technology, society, and culture which it must engage and accommodate.

LOT-EK's work to date has not been about stimulating vast changes in society and culture; rather it is about reflecting those changes through LOT-EK's own creative sensibilities. These are not the first European immigrants to arrive in North America and be excited and stimulated by what they have found there, consequently developing ideas that have reinvigorated its melting pot. Like all beginning architects, LOT-EK's partners have taken their work where they can find it, but they have been remarkably true to the design agenda they profess. Despite the fact that their work is primarily, to date, in art galleries and New York lofts, it is not pretentious. It is easily understandable and, it could be argued, derives more from the masses than the elite. LOT-EK refuses to get into overlong theoretical discussions about its work; its publications are refreshingly direct, pragmatic descriptions about how projects are made and what their intended functions are. LOT-EK uses a cinematic series of connected images and words to convey the context for its ideas, and though its drawings are intriguing, they are absolutely clear in communicating the nature of the object to be made. Another reason LOT-EK's work is accessible is because it is an art and an architecture that wants to be touched, climbed over and into, and most of all... used. It is tough, robust, made to be handled, and it looks like it. Though these objects now serve a new role, they have brought this pragmatic usability along with them, or rather, the designers have recognized that usability and worked hard not to excise it in the reusing process. Perhaps there is another way in which the WELCOME-BOX is a significant project. Sitting alone on that railway platform, open to the public twenty-four hours a day in a tough port city, it has a use and is in a location that is able to take full advantage of LOT-EK's design agenda — the establishment of an urban vernacular that is relevant, usable, and enjoyable.

FROM
HIGH-TECH
TO LOT-EK:
A BRIEF
JOURNEY
AROUND DABINSKY

Since standard shipping containers came into use in 1955, the
way things are shipped has radically altered our physical reality. The refinement of various standards for these steel boxes,
of which almost seven million are now moving around the world,
to two basic measurements (or variations of the TEU, Twentyfoot
Equivalent Standard) has defined the design of ships, railroad
cars, trucks, and cargo airplanes. It has also changed the landscape of ports, airports, and trucking yards. Bridges have been
raised to allow trains to ride with two rows of containers on
top of each other. Even packaging has adapted: cartons and bottles have shrunk or grown ever so slightly to optimize the amount
that can be fitted inside of a TEU container. From the small
scale of the beverages we drink, to the vast expanses taken up
by the "ghost ports" where three men can, with the help of
robots, load or unload a container ship with six thousand TEUs
in a matter of hours, containers have changed the contours of
the physical world we see around us.

The container is part of a wider system of distribution that
takes up a greater percentage of both our economic and our physical
space. Just-in-time inventory, the ready spread of information
through the internet and other electronic media, and the
increased mobility due to a finer grained transportation infrastructure conspire to create a situation in which the distribution
of an object or service is more important than its actual production. The result is a landscape in which giant "transshipment
centers," gargantuan airports and container ports, and the
plethora of small-scale distribution systems such as pickup
trucks are taking up an increasing amount of physical space.

Yet, the world of movement in which the container is king is
nearly invisible. We see only ephemeral projections in the world
of advertising, rather than the actual movement of the goods. We
rarely ever notice the containers as they race by us on the road,
and few of us ever visit a port. Outside of the shipping or packaging business, few care that the container rules so many
aspects of shape, size, and movement. It is up to artists or
architects to reveal these hidden measures of man's activities.
That task is one that Ada Tolla and Giuseppe Lignano have taken
on. The container has become their emblem, their project, and
their building block. By using the container, they have turned
what is invisible into a focal point, and have made what we use
to move things around into homes.

In doing so, they have found a way to keep alive a long tradition in architecture of revealing the emblematic elements of technology. They have done so by fusing the romance of industrial shapes with the love affair many architects have had with vessels of various sorts, from ships to Concordes. They have then given their new industrial expressions a larger cultural currency by designing them in a style that has become emblematic of the most appropriate way to live in large cities such as New York. The containers that figure so prominently in these architects' work serve to anchor a general investigation of the unnoticed and disused, the standardized, and that which is meant for production, not appearance. It brings into focus the texture of a background reality on which our daily lives float.

While this industrial romantic approach has roots in the eighteenth century, it did not become an important part of architecture until the latter half of the nineteenth century. When architects such as Eugène-Emmanuel Viollet-le-Duc began to incorporate new materials such as steel and glass into their work, they tried at first to subordinate these products of the industrial revolution to existing compositional models. It took designers from outside of the mainstream, such as Joseph Paxton and Gustave Eiffel, to create icons such as the Crystal Palace and the Eiffel Tower. When it became evident that such engineering marvels as bridges were far more powerful in their effect than buildings, architects began to aspire to making their designs as expressive (and large) as these utilitarian structures. They rarely succeeded at any scale, but they did begin to use elements from the world of engineering. Glass, steel, and concrete became not only constituent elements, but also part of the aesthetic of architecture. In the work of Dutch architects such as Gerrit Rietveld, Austrians such as Otto Wagner and Adolph Loos, and Americans such as (Austrian-born) Rudolf Schindler and Richard Neutra, domestic implements migrated from the kitchen, the boiler room, and the hardware store into the fabric of the house or office.

Thus, two strands emerged in modern architecture's approach to technology. While some architects continued to see their work as part of the construction of a new world on a vast scale and in tandem with engineers, others looked more toward the integration of architecture into the daily practice of modernization. Futurist and Constructivist architects dreamed of whole mountain ranges of concrete, proposed airports in the middle of cities, and drew their projects as vast abstractions whose elongated forms took little note of the small specks that were human beings meant to huddle inside these behemoths. At the Bauhaus, meanwhile, architects were trying to use new techniques of bending metal, plywood, and synthetics to create forms that would conform to the human body. They were using radiators and bare light bulbs without covering them up, so that users could understand and possibly even fix these implements of comfort. They employed scientific techniques such as motion study and statistics to create efficient spaces that would minimize human action. Instead of glorifying the new as larger than man, they tried to make novelty accessible and useful.

These attitudes came together in many architects' fascination with vessels. Le Corbusier lavished attention on airplanes, cars, and boats, the Futurists sought to blur buildings into sports cars, and American architects tried to adapt Raymond Loewy's "streamlining" into their buildings. They admired the engineering feats these vehicles represented: they were able to defy gravity in a way architecture could only dream of and made use of the bridges and roads whose scale was so thrilling. These cars, trains, and automobiles also represented the other side of an industrialized architecture: here, cold metal, knobs, and levers were an accepted part of the environment because they had to be. The demands for efficiency, speed, and safety were such that little of the covering that usually obfuscated the true way in which environments were heated, cooled, and even constructed could be present. As a result, these objects looked and smelled like technology.

The new profession of industrial design, spearheaded by Loewy along with such designers as Walter Teague, managed to control and exploit these intensive technologies. Cars, trains, boats, and, later, airplanes became sites for tremendous design innovation, but this success came at a price. Because industrial designers had to be so much closer to processes of manufacturing and, later, consumption patterns, they had little room to express, reveal, or develop a critical stance towards the objects they were forming. They also had little knowledge of space, light, texture, or most of the other basic elements architects had learned to manipulate to create complex environments. The result was a kind of built-in banality right below the shiny surfaces. But what surfaces they were! The car and truck invaded the city with their smooth, sculptural shapes. The world of motion undercut — sometimes literally — the stability of an architecture designed for the ages, and the storage devices for these machines, whether they were warehouses or parking garages, gave a lie to the careful articulations of conventional places of inhabitation.

On one level, architects failed miserably in their desire to adapt this look and feel to their buildings. They never managed to design structures as fast as cars or as expressive as industrial plants (though Albert Kahn did create grand factories). They usually had little or no role in the design of dams or bridges. Most clients rejected the overt presence of technology in their homes and workplaces, preferring such inventions as interior decorator Elsie De Wolfe's radiator covers. Where architects did succeed was in creating icons of frozen movement and production that stood outside of most people's experience: Brinkman and Van der Vlugt's Van Nelle Factory, Le Corbusier's Villa Savoye and William Van Alen's Chrysler Building come to mind. Architecture could not make the excitement of a new era of industrial production and continual movement inhabitable and recognizable, but it could make it iconic.

After the Second World War, architects stepped away from the attempt to make icons of modernization and concentrated on the building according to the systems they thought undergirded all this excitement (and terror). They felt that they could reveal the underlying truth on which the world of motion just floated, and thus reclaim the aesthetic and moral high ground for architecture. To most modernist designers, that meant using grids of various sorts. Over the years, these mathematical systems became more and more complex and more and more abstract. If they started out as constructional diagrams in the work of architects such as Ludwig Mies van der Rohe and Skidmore, Owings and Merrill, they quickly became purely mathematical grids that could be manipulated to create a campus, a city, or even a house. Once again, technology again faded into abstraction and out of people's lives.

It was not until the mid-1960s that the architects of Archigram in England, the Metabolists in Japan, and figures such as R. Buckminster Fuller and Paul Rudolph in the US tried to merge what they saw from the world of transportation into buildings. For Fuller, the Dymaxion House and the car had always been part of

the same research, but during this period he managed to gain
attention for his theories with the design of geodesic domes,
which made grids three-dimensional and inhabitable. The members
of Archigram dreamed of mobile living pods and other tools for
nomadic inhabitation. They imported construction methods and
consumer goods into the grids, turning them into ever-unfinished
cities. These communities were always growing and could, in some
cases, even move. The consumer's experience, not the method of
construction or the scale, was central in Archigram's methodology.
Underlying these dreams was the belief that the days of making specific objects for living in one place were coming to an end.
What was necessary instead was to adopt the systems of mass
production and economic organization to produce something like
a car in the manner of a car, but with the social and spatial
complexity of a building. Architects should use what they knew
about the making of comfortable, sensible environments to design
moving homes that could change, both in terms of location and
internally.

Again, they had little success. Their visionary schemes were
picked up by neither manufacturers nor the general public. At
most, they influenced the design of such specialized structures
as fair pavilions and tents, both of which leaned heavily on the
work of Buckminster Fuller, or temporary stage design, which put
the lessons of Archigram into practice. It turned out that the
wholesale adaptation of the forms of motion into architecture
was bound to fail because, by their very nature, these objects
were not designed to have a stable relationship to either the
human body or the surrounding context. They were isolated tools,
however beautiful they might be, or containers for those tools.

Those architects who accepted the built environment as the
starting point for design flexibility had more success.
Realizing that a form of mass production was responsible for a
stock of generic spaces that permitted at least internal movement, they began adapting industrial loft buildings for inhabitation. Their architecture acted as parasites and palimpsests on
the existing structural and mechanical systems, revealing the
generic forms into which one could plug a kitchen, a light, or
a bathroom without building defining walls. It was an architecture of renovation, of temporary inhabitation, and of flexibility.
Architects such as the late Alan Buchsbaum spearheaded the movement in New York, and soon it became a style documented in Joan

Kron's and Suzanne Slesin's 1978 book *High-Tech* and popularized by such films as Adrian Lyne's *9½ Weeks*. Here the grand dream of technological expression and production finally resolved itself to the adaptation of what existed outside of architecture so that it could be both livable and habitable. It didn't move and wasn't particularly moving, but it worked. For the first time in two hundred years, technological production became chic, affordable, and desirable.

It was into this situation that the partners of LOT-EK arrived when they came as postgraduates to Columbia University in 1990. They found the world of mainstream architecture still morose over the defeat of its technological dreams and caught in the throes of the controversies over Postmodernism. In response, they turned their eye to what was not considered architecture: the industrial vernacular in which they lived, and especially the elements of mobility that so fascinate most Europeans. It took Europeans, who had not grown up with the American adoration of technology as a distinct alternative to "home sweet home," which was seen as a respite from the restless movement so built into the native culture, to see the possibility of merging the escape from and to technology into one mode of architecture. American cars and trucks, especially, but also the elaborate systems that serviced these pieces of mobile technology, became the subject of their eyes and their cameras. They built up a lexicon of gas stations, truck stops, loading bays, storage spaces, signs, and the shiny vehicles themselves.

Their interest also coincided with a renewal of the belief that architecture had to address the technological challenge, though now because it was necessary to live with and wisely use our ability to make new forms and worlds, rather than because these achievements themselves were desirable. Architects had to make things that were comforting and comfortable and that made wise use of natural resources. Smart architecture was necessary. Thus, there was a renewed interest in groups such as Archigram, as well as in a search for an architecture that would consist of tactical insertions, instead of elaborate and systemic strategies. This latter approach was popularized in architecture schools such as SCI-Arc in Los Angeles, the Architectural Association in London, and Columbia University. Coming out of interpretations of poststructuralist theory, it was wary of anything that looked like a finished, fixed object, but also

refused to replace such buildings with clear systems. The frag-
ment, the unfinished, the guerilla-like, and the narrative took
precedent over the making of finished things. The architecture
and writing of Bernard Tschumi, Mark Wigley, Thom Mayne, Frank
Gehry, and Coop Himmelblau were especially important in this
trend. Younger architects such as Wes Jones, Neil Denari, and
Hani Rashid repopularized the notion of architecture as moveable
and moving technological assemblies by merging these theories
with the history of technological expressionism.

At the same time, a loose movement of architects was raiding the
parts bin. Some architects began importing actual mass-produced
fragments into their work in a way that was almost matter-of-
fact. Architects such as Smith-Miller + Hawkinson in New York,
Hodgetts + Fung Design Associates in Los Angeles, Kennedy &
Violich in Boston, and Will Bruder in Phoenix began to use plumbing
supplies, industrial fixtures, and electrical or mechanical
parts to make work that was both mechano-morphic and had a sense
of being integrated into existing conditions. This "Home Depot
Moderne" had its own roots in Frank Gehry's designs of the 1970s,
but evolved into an expressive use of the overabundance of materials that, first, mass market catalogues and, then, the internet
made much more available. These architects seemed to be indicating
that the contradiction between the home and the car could be dis-
solved, if one saw both of these not as whole objects, but as
collections of different parts that could exchanged. A hybrid architecture, half-building and half-car or -container, began to emerge.

LOT-EK, as Tolla and Lignano called themselves after setting up
practice in New York, merged many of these strands in the design
of a series of loft renovations and theoretical projects it
started in the second half of the 1990s. Tolla and Lignano raided
the parts bin for sinks that could become walls and made place
settings by using gaffer's tape. But what made their work
instantly recognizable was their use of tanks and containers.
They hit upon a building element that was in itself already part
of the industrial world, and yet was meant to contain things.
By importing it into the domestic sphere and cutting and past-
ing its various parts, they were able to turn it into a hybrid
of architecture and technology. The container and the shipping
vessel became the ultimate merger of everything architects were
trying to achieve. It was a building block, an expression of systems, a moveable bit of a changing society, and something that

could be found, rather than having to be constructed by using up resources.

LOT-EK was not the first firm to use containers. As early as 1966, Paul Rudolph had proposed towers for Manhattan in which these elements could become plug-in components. Architects working in Third World countries had used containers because they were efficient ways of quickly creating sheltered space. Students in architecture schools around the world turned out continual streams of container projects in which these humble TEUs provided shelter and constructional support. Temporary fairs and cafés used containers. There was thus a lexicon LOT-EK could use. What made the difference was Tolla and Lignano's willingness to take the container apart, to look at it as part of a family of other shipping means, such as tanker trucks, and to insert it into the New York domestic environment already primed for technological implements by the high-tech movement.

It was the fragments of a moveable and industrially produced family of forms, in other words, that became the elements in LOT-EK's lexicon. It is only in its more visionary projects, such as the Goree Memorial and Museum (Figs. 1, 2) of 1997 and the MDU (mobile dwelling unit) proposal of 1999, that the container states its iconic functions. These visions act as the validators for the collection of fragments with which LOT-EK usually works, providing a prospective model towards which the lofts and temporary installations are building.

Figs. 1, 2: Goree Memorial
and Museum
Dakar, Senegal, 1997

As such, Tolla and Lignano were able to use containers and the other paraphernalia of a technological world with a great deal of success exactly because much of their work remained within the realm of visions, and they could clearly state the promise they felt was inherent in these modules. By the time they started working, the notion that art could be an environment, that art could be temporary, and that architecture could also be art and time-based, was accepted in at least the New York art scene. The integration of technology into such environments was accepted because they were not meant to be places of comfortable inhabitation. They were rather meant to make us aware of, or tell a story about, our or the artist's daily life.

Tolla and Lignano also benefited from an emerging interest in architecture as a form of temporary installation, which itself is a reflection of a culture in which mobile and time-based appearances take precedence over permanent, crafted objects. They made their mark with such structures as the 1998 TV-TANK (see p. 67) and the 2000 MIXER (see p. 68), as well as with installations for the Brooklyn Academy of Music (1996-98), the Whitney Museum of American Art (1999), and the UCLA Armand Hammer Museum (2001). In all of these projects, the industrial fragments served as both conduits for media and temporary places of inhabitation. Divorced from what we usually think of as functional spaces, as well as from the need to respond to a context, they were free to express the very fact that all of our constructions today are essentially defined by and about motion. As architecture reduces itself more and more to either functional implements or background construction, it is only in the moments that serve to frame highly precious objects — stores, apartments for rich people, art spaces — that a container in which the use of any amount of resources are permitted makes sense. How to make such precious containers is something architects learned from those who had learned from the extra-architectural fields spawned by technology: fair pavilions, stages, exhibition designs, and art itself, which took as its task the revealing of our world within its own means.

Even LOT-EK's dwelling units, such as the 2000 Morton loft (see p. 68), have the quality of installation projects, not just in the sense that they carry on the tradition of industrial-language renovations of loft spaces, but because their very forms borrow from the "art tradition." The tanks that form their centerpiece draw attention to themselves as rarefied objects, and the owner admits (gladly) to adjusting his manner of using the environment to this sacred object, by ducking his head, folding himself into the containers' narrow confines, and otherwise working with these imported fragments, rather than using them merely for their functional purposes. Similarly, the bric-a-brac attitudes developed in the Guzman penthouse (Fig. 3) of 1996 and the various environments LOT-EK has made for itself cite and display a tradition of assemblage that, in the end, is more related to the walk-through environments first developed by artists such as Ed Kienholz and Claes Oldenburg than it is to domestic architecture.

It is therefore not coincidental that most of LOT-EK's influence — a result, as always, of media exposure — has come not through

Fig. 3: Guzman Penthouse
New York, 1996
photo: © Paul Warchol

the application of its craft to the making of humble abodes, but
through its associations with such events as the Whitney
Biennial (1999), fundraising dinner settings, and art galleries
for Henry Urbach (2000) and Sara Meltzer (2000). Not only do
thousands of people see these spaces, but here architecture is
free to have the function of being about something, a privilege
we usually accord to art. In their most visionary projects, such
as the Goree Memorial and Museum of 1997, Tolla and Lignano
dreamed of extending the logic of art into the public realm. It
is exactly its unbuilt and visionary quality that has made it a
powerful part of the art tradition, as it is free to act as an
image, rather than being an occupied and thus relative part of
our experience.

Finally, we can also see LOT-EK's work in relation to the wider
acceptance of the world of motion and distribution in the world
of architecture. Once the computer had reduced information and
imagery to interchangeable bits, the designer was free to treat
all data as equal and build up forms from these abstract elements.
The same computer can produce a car and a building, and more and
more we demand the same access to technology in those formerly
disparate objects. The container became the symbol for the "dumb
box" to which the miniaturization endemic to digital technologies reduced buildings, cars, and the computer itself. Not final
form, but the collection of information, its organization, and its
(temporary) storage became the tasks of the architect. Firms such
as MVRDV in the Netherlands thus logically developed from "data
mining" and "data scapes" to proposing a complete Container City
in 2001 made out of five thousand containers.

This, then, is the context in which the work of LOT-EK emerges
and functions. Its work is the heir to a long and lively tradition that is marked mainly by failures to make technology an
integral part of architecture. It is also a response to an
acceptance of technology as part of the fabric of everyday life.
It is a recognition of the importance of one aspect of technology, namely standardized shipping and storage, in defining a
reality we rarely see. It uses the container to sum up these
fragmentary technologies and to celebrate the transformation of
our world into one of continual motion and distribution. In
recent work, Tolla and Lignano seem to be moving towards a more
subtle and insertive way of making their moves. They seem to be
sublimating what they have learned from the container, from the

car, from the computer, and from the culture in which these technologies shape our lives into forms whose impact is subtler and
therefore, perhaps, more profound.

Everywhere around us things move, people move, data moves. As we
sit in our chairs at home or work, or as we buzz along in our
various vehicles, we tend to lose track, perspective, and sense
of all that flux. LOT-EK makes us aware of a world in motion and
at home in its perpetually shifting contours.

Christopher Scoates: Experimental work in the field of portable architecture has a rich and important history. From the Vienna-based Missing Link, to Ant Farm in the US, to Archizoom of Florence, to EAT (Experiments in Art and Technology) of New York, to Events Structures Research Group of Amsterdam, to Archigram of London, architects have been concerned with throwaway architecture and buildings that could be transferred from one place to another. Can you talk about where you see yourself fitting into this history?

Giuseppe Lignano: We have gone about this topic — throwaway or mobile architecture — more or less like artists would, which basically means that we have built these things, at first with our own hands, or we have had them built later (like we'll do with the MDU), as things that are going to exist for real. That, I believe, makes a huge difference both from a programmatic point of view and from a material point of view. The "material approach" has also helped us develop a much less polished, designer-like methodology with results that are more hybrid — existing objects that come together, collide, if you will, almost to materialize a desire. In fact, our interest in using pre-existing objects (products) to be transformed into new pro-grams (products) is also a very important aspect of our research that is "new." The fact that our projects are made out of already existing objects places them in a different epoch, where the stress is not only in designing architecture that "looks and feels" like industrial/technological products, to touch on what Aaron says in his essay, but it is actually made out of them. It is a more thorough acceptance and understanding of who we are — a "product" society — and, for us, there is a liberating effect of seeing the richness of stimuli and potential of our civi-lization, which, although largely untapped, could reveal a lot of creative aspects or alternatives to the generally negative and drab view of our consumer-based civilization.

CS: Ada, can you elaborate on your statement that your reuse of industrial objects has less to do with recycling and more to do with ideas about containment?

Ada Tolla: The reason why we use existing containers and exist-ing objects in particular is not because we are interested in recycling and environmental issues as a first concern. Although we are very happy that they have come along with what we are doing, we are more interested in the creative process that develops in working with existing objects. Dealing with forms, volumes, textures, structures, colors, and the many inputs that an existing object offers is what we find very compelling at a creative level. Of course, the choice of many of the objects that we've used is not casual. It is based on our interest in objects that are, on one hand, extremely banal and representative of contemporary culture, but, on the other hand, have a very strong volumetric, almost architectural, value — objects like containers, that contain volumes, also modular objects. Essentially, we're interested in the idea of generating architecture starting from simple, existing forms and volumes that can be combined, reconfigured, or transformed.

CS: At first glance, some of your work appears to be a cross between *Barbarella*, *Blade Runner*, and a techno-utopia, but on closer inspection, reveals a deep concern with beauty and function. Can you address this?

GL: We are definitely interested in pushing the uses, the functions, of modern gadget-like things toward something that is simultaneously more contemporary and futuristic. Of course, our approach is different than that used in movies. We do it with an awareness of something that is going to be lived in, that is real. We either start from the briefings and the program that is given to us by a client, or things that we make up ourselves or that we want to push, but there is always a very strong relationship between the way things appear and the way things function. As far as our idea of beauty is concerned, I would say that it's not so much about creating the aesthetic of the future. We push to derive our aesthetics from the way that we address function, space, and everything that concerns architecture per se. In other words, our interest is never to apply a veneer, a beautification or a decoration on top of more conceptual or more functional and spatial qualities that the project has. Beauty needs to be derived from these qualities. Our deep idea of beauty is about questioning. We hope that people can relate to our products or to our projects not by judging how harmonious or classically beautiful they are, but by how provocative they are.

CS: You have said that your work addresses "the interaction of the human body with products and byproducts of industrial and technological culture." What inspired you to investigate such an idea?

AT: Our primary interest is starting from the products and byproducts of both industrial and technological culture, from the containers and the televisions, to the way that technology has impacted our world. That is the world we take from, the world we import into our architecture. The interaction of the human body with that world is something that we started investigating from the beginning. It comes from playing with these objects that are not designed by us, but that are sort of given. There is a strange imposition that is generated. On one hand, there is a suggestion of how a body can occupy those objects, but, on the other hand, there is almost an imposition or a series of obstacles that then become interesting spatial solutions. Ultimately, we are interesting in placing a human body inside one of these containers and seeing what ways you can solve program functions using the container itself. Giuseppe has a very good analogy, which is that these objects are a little bit like a whale, a beached whale! The idea of taking these containers and then trying to address with one object all the programmatic functions that we are given within one determined project and, of course, the way in which all these functions respond to how the body is supposed to use them is very interesting. We are fascinated by the fact that there is always a question mark, and we don't really know what the final solution will be until we manipulate the object itself.

GL: I also want to comment on the word "inspired" that you use in your question. The inspiration comes from our observation of ways in which this thing already happens. It happens in very marginal aspects of our civilization, like in the Third World, where people reuse objects all the time and make them into something completely new. It happens also in our First World society in more random situations like construction sites and temporary constructions where people transform objects and occupy objects that are not generally "occupiable," so to speak. Of course, after being inspired by observing how these things already happen in random ways all over the globe, we developed a more personal way of doing this. Ada and I have developed a way of looking at these objects so that when we encounter them, we immediately begin to sense what these objects could become. We find daily inspiration in objects, materials, and systems that we see around us.

CS: Do you think it is possible to make buildings that are not merely about function and utility, but also contain ideas about society?

AT: Well, one wants to say that in making buildings that are about functions and utility, one is already expressing ideas about society. But I think that, in our particular case, we choose to do marginal but very penetrating work about our contemporary urban environment. I think it expresses something about our society, about the social layering, about environmental issues, and so on. I think that one can touch on a larger picture even within the immediate programmatic issues of one project. Of course, one thing that I'm thinking about is the idea that we find our work to be very grounded in the urban scan. It is the idea that this very large investigation touches all the different points of our environment. They are not points that one wants to see necessarily, and they are not points that belong to architecture necessarily, but we take them into architecture. So, to me, that process expresses something about the society in which we live.

GL: What Ada said is very important. The thrust of Pop Art and other expressions of that kind is the idea of commenting on our civilization by reusing things that we produce, things that we take for granted, things that we don't want to see. Although they are considered add-ons, these things constitute so much more of the built environment than things designed by architects ever have.

CS: Many of your works blur the boundaries between art, architecture, and entertainment. Stylistically, your installations have a very theatrical and/or "rock n' roll" sensibility. I can see your work being suited to stage design. Have you ever considered this as a possible venue for your work?

GL: We have only had one little experience with this when a friend of ours, who is a set designer, invited us to contribute one of the seven different sets that he was developing for a two-song video for A Tribe Called Quest. We had a lot of fun doing it; it's definitely a great thing to do. Of course, we would like to do it more our own way, which, as I was saying about the *Barbarella* and *Blade Runner* issue, is more architectural and less about decoration and creating just a visual fiction, although we realize the importance of creating more spectacular and theatrical real things. Of course our architecture and installations already have something theatrical about them, but creating something for the theater, or for television or the movies, is a completely different endeavor. The only other experience that we have had is creating installations for very short events at BAM (the Brooklyn Academy of Music) and other institutions that were still real events with people. They were not being broadcast or filmed and, therefore, the fiction and visionary elements are very different, but they still were great experiences.

AT: One thing I want to add to what Giuseppe is saying is that the major appeal of this kind of project is that its nature is completely different from that of conventional architectural projects. The concept of a project as a temporary thing, which will only last for a very limited amount of time, is very intriguing and follows completely different rules than conventional architectural thought. It is interesting for us also because we are continuously looking at temporary conditions within the urban environment as things that, as temporary as they are, are permanent in the sense that they are always present.

GL: I think that it would be very interesting to do what George Lucas did with his first movie, *THX 1138*, where he basically shot everything on location and picked strange shots of common things, like a parking garage or a series of telephone booths, to create something futuristic. It would be very interesting to use our visions of the urban scan as something to be shot on location, maybe shooting a whole movie in a container depot town like Elizabeth, New Jersey, for example.

CS: Do you see your installations functioning simply as art/architecture or would you like to see them inspire mass-market design?

AT: We have always been very interested in the idea of making products or producing mass-market design out of architecture. When we started the MDU and other previous projects, the idea of possibly developing architecture that one could sell through a catalogue was something we consistently found interesting. It is obviously deeply rooted in American culture, and it brings the kind of architecture that one could see as a very conceptual or theoretical kind of speculation into a much more tangible and accessible realm.

GL: The idea of mass-market design is very interesting at the level of architectural products like the MDU, or other projects like the AMERICAN DINER or even the MIXER. I guess every project we've done that is contained in an object has been thought of as something that could become a product. We think that there is a possibility of doing something like that. There are many realms in which you can think about it, like adding a bathroom to a house, or the moveable house or office that could be seen more as a complete architecture and sold as a product. We are very fascinated by that, not only because it is so much part of our culture — the idea of buying things through a catalogue, or over the internet now — but also because of the type of work that we do. We are interested in sifting through pre-existing products, like a container or a cement mixer, that could serve as valuable spaces to be transformed architecturally. Make that transformation, create something, and then place it again in the marketplace — that would definitely be a major accomplishment.

CS: You feel at home in galleries. In fact, you have developed several works specifically for museums and galleries that push the boundaries of architecture and installation art. How do you see yourselves negotiating the balance of architecture as installation?

GL: I would say that the way we see architecture per se is as a giant installation. We decompose every project we do even on a very large scale in that manner, because of the objects that we generally use, and because we see architecture as an assembly of objects and systems. We don't really separate the two moments — the moment we are installing something in a gallery and the moment we are building something in the street from the ground up. Of course there is a difference in the materials that you use, how temporary something will be, the structure, and so on. I would say that it is more than negotiating the balance of architecture as installation. It is something that happens in architecture all the time, from the moment you start seeing it both as a creative endeavor and as a practical endeavor that needs to deal with structure, legal issues, permits, etcetera. I think what is interesting about your question is the whole relationship between art and architecture and, specifically in our work, the moment we are hired as architects and the moment we are doing something as artists. We mediate that in our minds, and for us it's all the same process. If the installation in the gallery means that we do not have a real program given by a customer or a client, we basically make it up; we create our own idea of what that program should be. On the other hand, when we face a more practical and real architectural project, our effort is one of not being burdened completely by the program, but using it as a springboard for our creativity, our imagination, and also our criticism of the typical architectural program, and hopefully arriving at more interesting conclusions.

CS: You have used a cement mixer, a petroleum tanker, and an airline-shipping container. What industrial objects do you wish to use in the future?

AT: There are objects that we have used in projects that haven't been built. They have stayed in our mind and we hope that it's just a matter of time before we get to use them. One of them, of course, is an airplane fuselage. As you know, we have done a project for the University of Washington using a 747 and got very close to building it, but at the end it was cancelled. So that is something we are definitely interested in. I would say there has always been the desire to grow into bigger and bigger objects. Another project that we developed was a huge municipal water tank used for an indoor skateboard park. So there is desire to put our hands on very large objects that already exist. But also there is an interest in exploring things that can be repeated and, through the repetition, can create something. We've been looking at a lot of concrete tanks, tubs, and boxes that are very much part of heavy-duty construction, like sewage systems. Those are interesting because they are very formative, but they are all different sizes, and what is interesting is the way in which those different sizes can be combined. Things like concrete forms are generally just of service to the construction industry and don't belong to the final product. It is interesting to investigate whether it is possible to actually use these objects to make them become final forms, final schemes, final systems, in the construction of real architecture.

GL: I'd like to add that we are always looking for new things, always observing, and it's always a surprise. We know that there are a number of heavy duty or specific objects and systems in a lot of different industries that are not used in architecture but that we would love to use. I remember Lisa Norton's big ducted work in the *Climate Control: Mechanical Systems as Bodily Experience* show that you did in 1996 when you were at the Atlanta College of Art Gallery. We had a project that was not realized this past winter for an apartment where everything was created with ducts. The idea was to blow up the size of regular air ducts so that they could be inhabited by people as corridors and hallways, or by other objects as storage. There are many possibilities; we see it as an infinite world.

CS: You have also used recycled plastic containers like detergent bottles to make lamps and other objects. How were these projects developed and what were your primary concerns?

AT: Those were very early projects that we reflect on with a lot of enthusiasm and fondness, because they were extremely naive and we approached them like kids. They are interesting because, even on a very tight and small scale, they already convey a similar vision and approach to what we currently have. It was very much about discovery. Part of it, I think, was that we were enamored of the American pop world. The Tide bottles and other detergent bottles on a supermarket shelf were very fascinating to us — the logos, the colors, the branding, and so on. We were interested in trying to incorporate all of those elements into design, upscaling these objects into another world, simply placing another technological element like the electrical bulb inside one of these plastic containers, and then watching the little miracle that happens when you turn it on. There is this fantastic colored light that creates a mood. It's not a reading light, but something more, something special. And up to this day, people who come into our studio or into our homes and see these lights are always very fascinated. People react on all sorts of levels because the objects are so ordinary; they are in our faces every single day, but it's as if we've never seen them before. We are seeing them in a new light, as it were.

GL: When we were making them, we felt that we were basically making cartoons—the old-fashioned Hanna-Barbera cartoons with lots of yellow, orange, red, and those kinds of Technicolor colors.

CS: How do you see the role of humor in your work?

AT: It's fundamental, what else can I say? It's crucial, and I don't think it's accidental that this question happens right after discussing the plastic container lights, because I think that the playfulness that started on a smaller scale with the idea of color is very much present in our work and not necessarily embraced by the typical architect. The other thing is the idea that one can, to some extent, attach humor to something that is conceptual, theoretical, abstract, or intellectual. I think that also is a very important element for us, the idea that complicated things don't have to be boring.

GL: I think that the question about humor reconnects to your original question about beauty. My answer to your question about beauty, again, was that we do not conceive of beauty as harmony, balance, and the classical aspects of beauty. Rather, we see beauty more as a quality that provokes something in the viewer, which I think is basic to the contemporary or modern sense of beauty in art. Humor is a part of that. It's one of those things you can provoke in people. It is definitely something that we remember feeling and we still feel when we see ways in which people reuse objects in particular situations like, as I was saying before, maybe on a beach in Jamaica or on a construction site. When you see a chair made out of whatever, or a truck that becomes an office, for example, it's always full of humor because it's basically full of surprise. That is great and that is what we love.

CS: Music, computer games, film, and TV play a large role in your work. What is the significance of popular culture in your work?

GL: Popular culture absolutely plays a large role. As we said previously, we actually want to add something to popular culture, bring something to the foreground to make people more conscious of what comprises our contemporary environment, just like Warhol's *Campbell's Soup Cans* made people aware of the importance of advertising in American life or in contemporary Western life. The role of TV and all entertainment is even greater, being even more a part of our contemporary society. I can remember discussing this with Robert Kronenburg in Liverpool, and he said, "I think it's interesting to compare what you do now with how people in the '60s and '70s were importing technology and entertainment to their art. Now people are so much more used to it. It's so much less threatening and works much more as a hook, as something that actually attracts people to explore new ideas in architecture." Going along with that, I should mention that we have used, for instance, TV in TV-TANK more as bait to attract people to experience a space like the interior of a tank than in any other way. That was the most important role that the TV set was playing in there. It was the same thing with the MIXER; it was a play between the two things, but definitely the larger role was to attract people to experience a space like a mixer. So there is a whole exploitive use that we make of popular culture, TV, and entertainment in general.

CS: Moveable buildings are a valuable, if comparatively unrecognized, component of the built environment. Clearly the MDU could be used for everything from disaster relief, commerce, education, medicine, manufacturing, and entertainment, to low-income housing. How do you see the MDU being used?

GL: The MDU was designed as a model dwelling unit. We envisioned the individual or the couple that would move around the globe for different reasons, not necessarily glamorous ones like Naomi Campbell might, but for other more mundane and normal reasons. We think that will happen more in the future. We are thinking how many more people will be moving around for a number of months or will desire to have a home away from home that can be moved everywhere. So maybe you will have your private residence in London or New York or wherever, but when you move around the globe you will always have something that travels before you with all your belongings set up already. We have always thought of the MDU as something flexible that could be customized just like you customize a car, adding new stuff or changing the colors. The other way of looking at the MDU's use is like you were saying about disaster relief, commerce, education, and so on. There is definitely a way of creating the same kind of experience that we have created with the MDU, but with another use in mind. I'm sure that the moment we start thinking about a different object, still made out of a container, let's say, for disaster relief, it definitely will be different. Say you want a place for a lot of people just to sleep and shower and nothing else and they're not going to do any real cooking. These could be more or less variations on the MDU, or they could be brand new projects. The only thing they will have in common is that maybe they use a container, but they would be called something else, "EDU" or something like that.

AT: I'd like to touch on the idea of the low-income housing. Now that we are in the development phase of the MDU, we are thinking of it as some sort of housing that is neither low-income nor high-income. It's just housing. It's done totally in the spirit of a product that could be mass-marketed —

GL: And they could have different variations, be more luxurious or less luxurious, depending on one's budget, but start from a standard form and program.

CS: You have developed a number of works where shipping containers are transformed into functional spaces like a diner, a museum, and now a home. What inspired you to investigate the use of containers in your work?

GL: Well, just consider the omnipresence and abundance of containers on this planet! They've become maybe the most ubiquitous objects of that size and of those qualities. Everywhere we look there are shipping containers. They are great objects. They are very easy. They're like building blocks, they can be colorful, and they're strong. We thought we could take advantage of them. Since the very beginning of working together as LOT-EK, we started thinking about using containers. The biggest push was given by the project for Africa —

AT: Which started from a visit to one of the big container sites in Jersey. It had a very strong impact, I think, on our work from that moment on, because we were in a space that was completely defined by containers and had a very powerful urban quality. There were big squares, piazzas, avenues, streets with perpendicular little alleys, and so on. We felt like we were inside a city and even commented on that. I think that was very much the beginning of understanding the potential of these masses of containers, which is also the potential of what happens in ports when we see these huge walls that keep growing and expanding. The one thing that I would add is the idea that the container can be used both for internal space and the quality obtained from stacking them one on top of the other. You have one particular kind of spatial experience when you act within the container, and you have another one when you start stacking containers and generating architecture just by doing that —

GL: Creating walls of containers, using containers as very large bricks to define large spaces.

CS: There is a current trend, a growing emphasis in American culture, on housewares, and the decoration and maintenance of our domestic environment. Magazine racks are rife with shelter magazines, home stores like Crate and Barrel, Pottery Barn, and IKEA are booming, and Home Depots are the size of the UK. What kind of influence does this have on your current work? Do you think the MDU subconsciously plays into this mass nesting instinct?

GL: Well, the trend that we'd love to take more advantage of is that, finally, it seems as though American culture is rediscovering modern architecture and contemporary design, and is leaving behind a little bit of the whole folksy Pottery Barn-look of a few years ago. It is good just to create against a sort of blank canvas, starting from scratch, and rediscovering modern values both aesthetically and functionally. Consider what happened with the publication *Wallpaper**: it's helped to make a historical style out of modernism, but, at the same time, has relaunched some ideas about modern living that are very important. We hope those ideas will catch on at a deeper level, especially the notion of a bigger scale of architecture, since most of the architecture being built in the States right now is still very much in the wake of the Postmodernism of the '80s, with colonnades, fringes, bricks, Victorian styles, and bric-a-brac all over the place. As far as what the MDU has to do with all of that, I don't know. I guess maybe it is the fact that people are rediscovering more modern aesthetics and the value of modern design which was about building everything into things and maybe making things move and making things functional. Definitely the MDU is very much in that direction and it could definitely take advantage of that.

AT: I especially like your inclusion of Home Depot in the list of references that you gave. It was, for Giuseppe and me, a huge discovery when we first came here. The Do-It-Yourself idea is very much an Anglo-Saxon thing that is completely absent in our Italian background. More than that, there's the idea that many of the places you mentioned belong to a network, making it possible for you to move throughout the States, perhaps around the globe, and find yourself in places that are completely identical, that all serve the exact same purpose. So, in that sense, I think there is also a link with what we are trying to do and with the idea of an architecture that is not just a one-of-a-kind place in one position, but has the potential for repetition and variation in a global network.

GL: Maybe Home Depot could carry the MDU very soon, who knows, right? Together with the fantastic array of garage doors that you see as soon as you get there, outside of the big shed that Home Depot is. Maybe in the parking lot? MDU-Model I, MDU-Model II, and MDU-Model III. Why not?

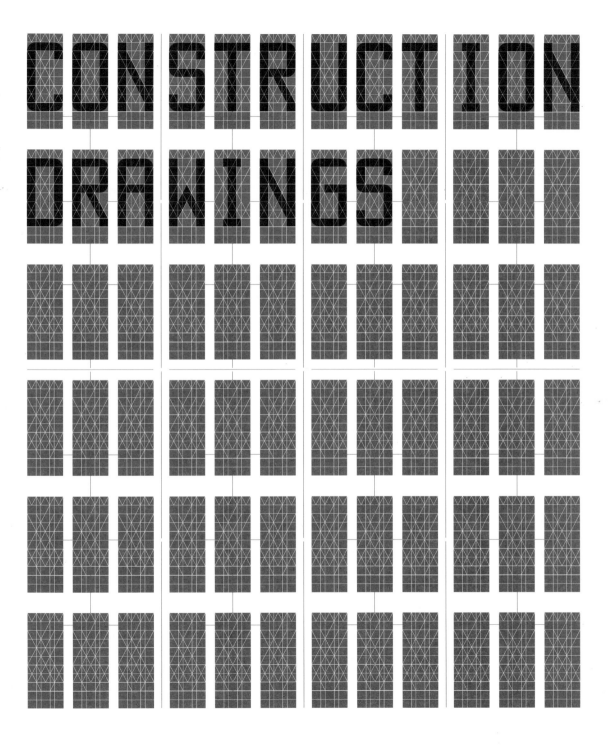

CONSTRUCTION DRAWINGS

CLOSET

KITCHEN

SOFA

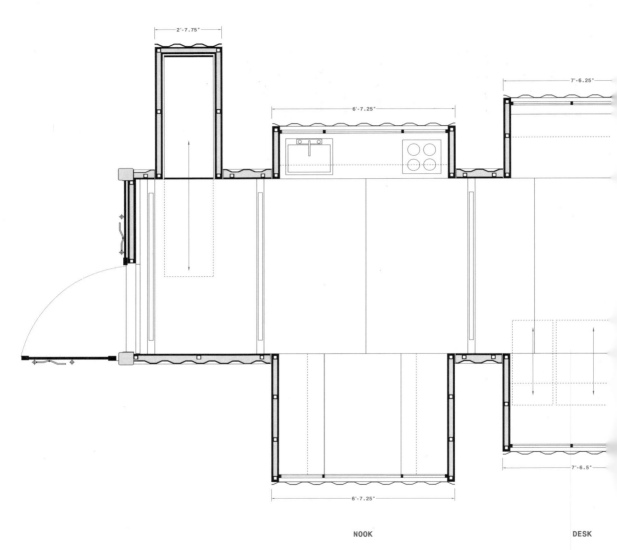

NOOK

DESK

SHOWER   SINK   TOILET

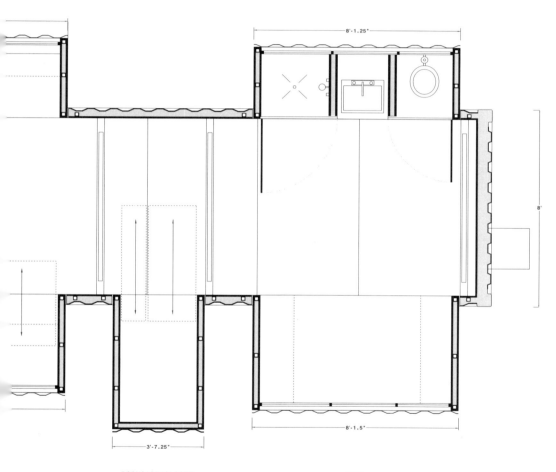

8'-1.25"

8'

8'-1.5"

3'-7.25"

BOOKCASE/CLOSET   **BED**

CLOSET   KITCHEN   SOFA

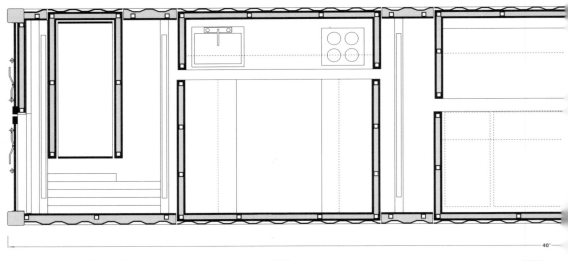

40'

FLOOR PANELS   NOOK   DESK

FLOOR PANELS   SHOWER   SINK   TOILET

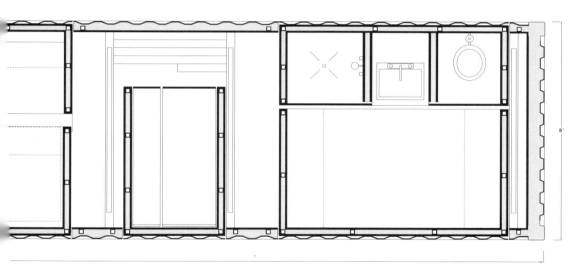

8'

BOOKCASE/CLOSET   BED

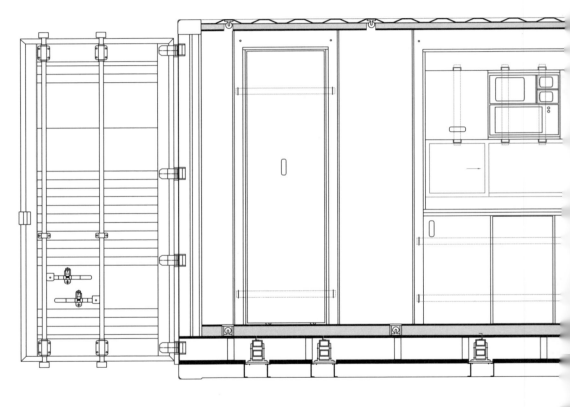

CLOSET

KITCHE

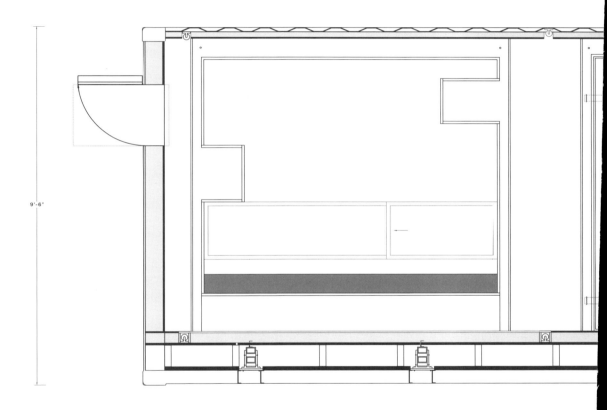

9'-6"

BED

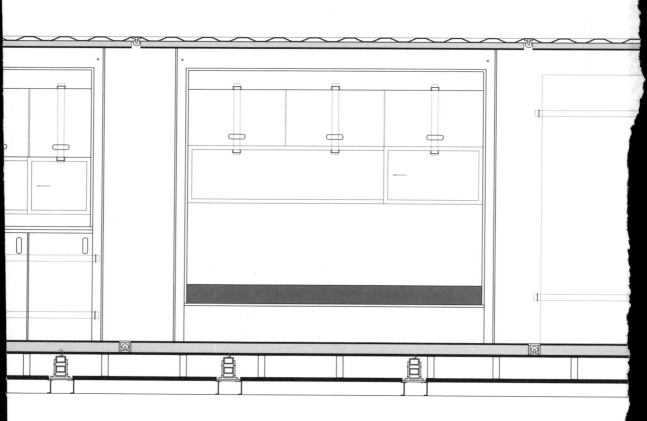

SOFA

FLOOR P

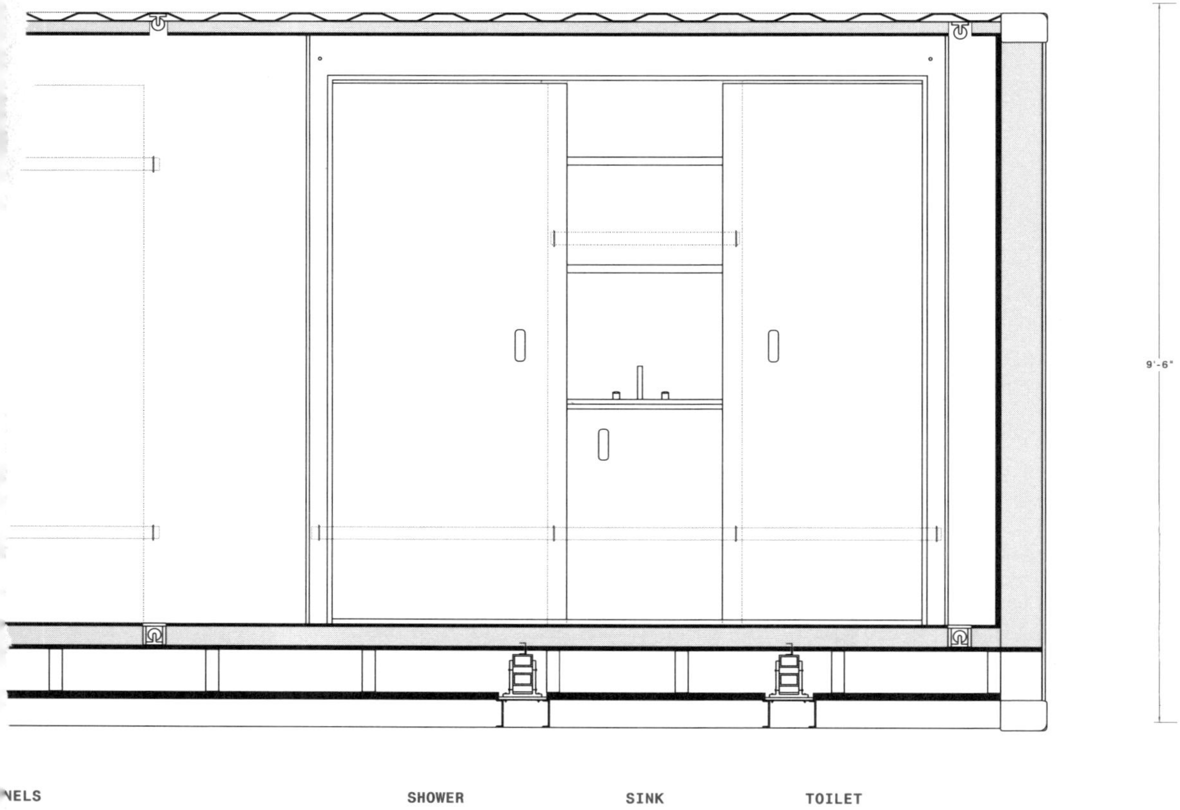
9'-6"
NELS
SHOWER
SINK
TOILET

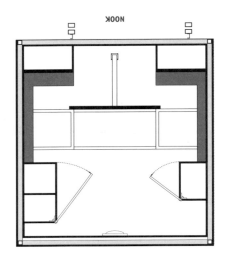

NOOK

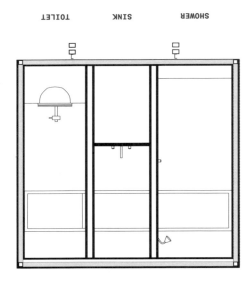

SHOWER　　　SINK　　　TOILET

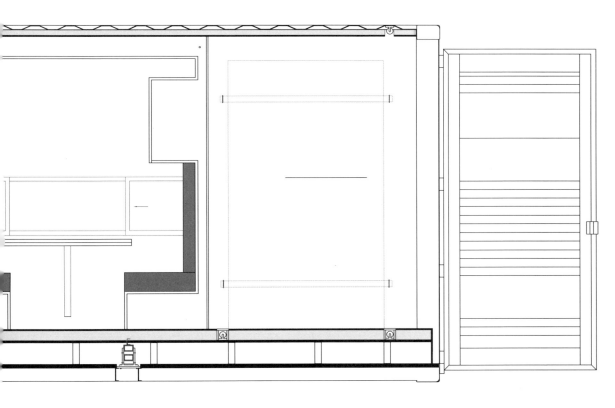

NOOK   FLOOR PANELS

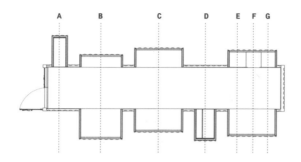

A B C D E F G

SECTION A

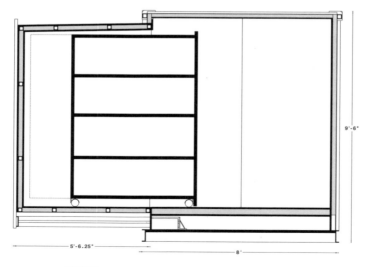

9'-6"

5'-6.25"

8'

CLOSET

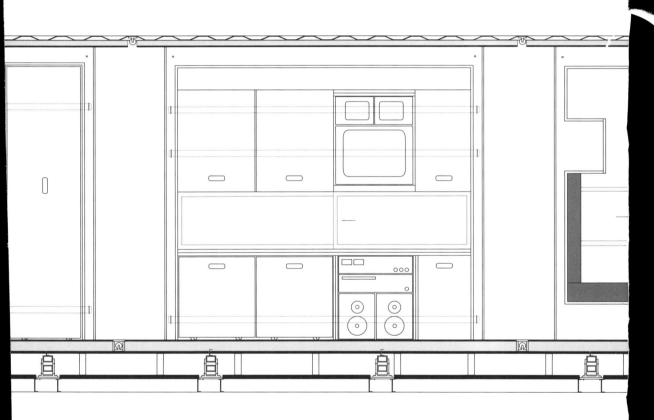

OOKCASE / CLOSET   DESK

SECTION B

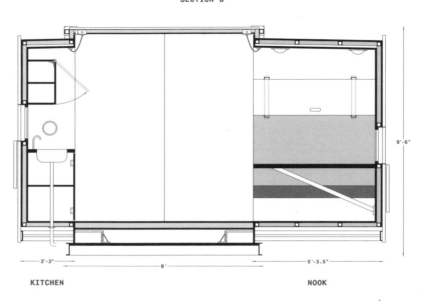

9'-6"

2'-2" 8' 5'-3.5"

KITCHEN   **NOOK**

SECTION C

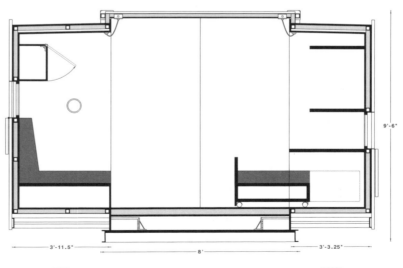

9'-6"

3'-11.5" 8' 3'-3.25"

SOFA   **DESK**

SECTION D

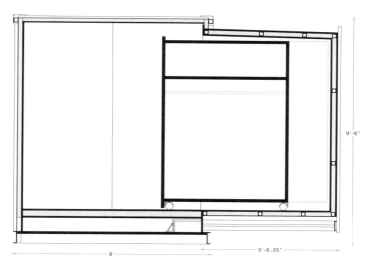

9'-6"

8'

5'-6.25"

BOOKCASE/CLOSET

SECTION E

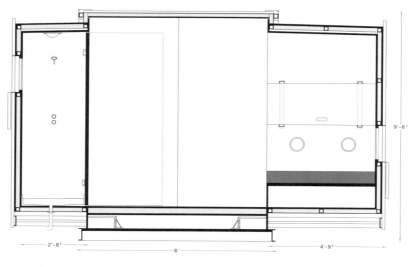

9'-6"

2'-8"

8'

4'-9"

SHOWER

BED

SECTION F

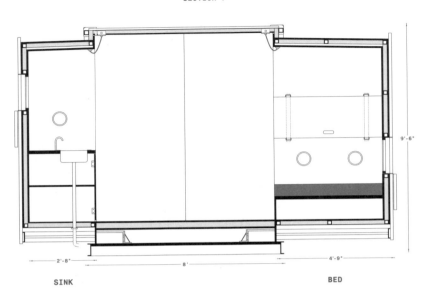

9'-6"

2'-8"   8'   4'-9"

SINK   BED

SECTION G

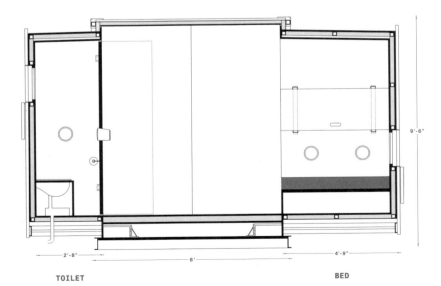

9'-6"

2'-8"   8'   4'-9"

TOILET   BED

MDU

FABRICATION

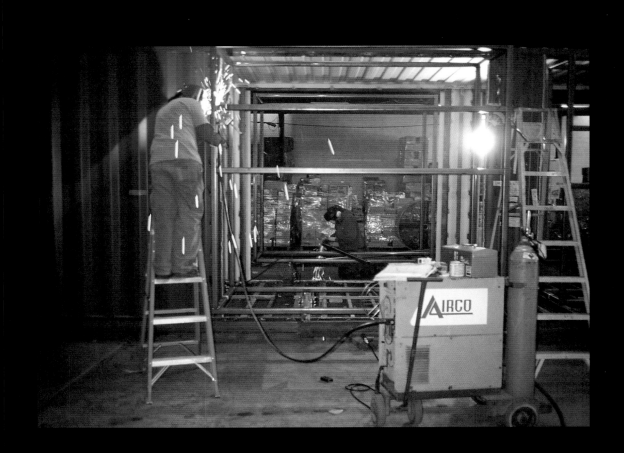